As always, Jack

May 2,

Beebe, darling,

I was just finishing up on the letter to you thanking you for the picture and sex when all of a sudden somebody drops two more letters from you in my lap. After blushing and thanking him, I find that one of them is from Jax (no kin to the beer of the same name), dated March 18, and is the most enjoyable piece of literature I ever read. I mean the one where you said you thought it was peachy of me to be in love of you and that you might even possibly might be the same. Obviously the girl got too much of that Florida sun, I says to myself after picking myself up off the floor. But it's wonderful to think about, and I feel like my head is up there at about 10,000 feet in the clouds. All I've got to say is, it couldn't have happened to

A WARTIME LOVE STORY

As always, Jack

EMMA SWEENEY

BACK BAY BOOKS

Little, Brown and Company

Boston   New York   London

Originally published in hardcover by Little, Brown and Company, April 2002

First Back Bay paperback edition, April 2003

Library of Congress Cataloging-in-Publication Data

Sweeney, Emma.

As always, Jack : a wartime love story / by Emma Sweeney.

p. cm.

ISBN 0-316-75858-2 (hc) / 0-316-73871-9 (pb)

1. Sweeney, John Milton — Correspondence. 2. United States. Navy — Officers — Correspondence. 3. Air pilots, Military — United States — Correspondence. 4. Sweeney, Beebe Mathewson — Correspondence. 5. Navy spouses — United States — Correspondence. 6. Sweeney family. 7. Sweeney, Emma. 8. Love-letters. I. Title.

V62 .S94 2002

359'.009'273 — dc21

[B]   2001038838

10 9 8 7 6 5 4 3 2 1

Designed by Michelle McMillian

Q-FF

Printed in the United States of America

To my father

"They came to me soundlessly, like the waters of a spring, and in the beginning I could not understand the sweetness that was invading me. There was neither voice nor vision, but the presentiment of a presence, of a warmth very close and already half guessed."

— from *Wind, Sand and Stars*,
by Antoine de Saint-Exupéry

was in love with you. It expla...
...I guess things that have been p...
...or instance, why I write you...
...letters, why I think about you...
...he day and dream about you...
...he night, and why I'm so eager...
...ack to the...with your f...
...tution (w...work so g...
...ores) you...ow it all...
...ough. And...is great lo...
...ue for ya...me any...
...which is u...but you...
...now I'll n...nything at...
...hese twelve...ween Dec. 29...
...an. 9 (Check?) only two months ag...
...t was that we were in the...
...wl, the Biltmore Bowl, and, a...
...ter, the Boysenberry Bowl.

...The amazing thing about it is...
...ing of coincidences that set up...

Part One

WHEN I WAS ABOUT TEN years old I was nosing around in some boxes in the basement of my family's house in Coronado, California, when I discovered a large manila envelope marked "Navy Department, Bureau of Naval Personnel: Official Business." Inside I found a photograph of my father, a certificate attesting to his death during active service to his country, and a letter. I had never seen a picture of my father before.

I felt as though I were looking in a mirror. Here were the same deeply set eyes as my own, and dark, wide eyebrows. My mother's own Scandinavian looks — blonde hair, blue eyes, and fair skin — were more evident in my older brothers. Most important to me, however, was the typed letter, written days before his plane went down and addressed to my

3

mother. I read the letter several times, looking for some clue in it that he knew about me. Did he know I existed?

I never told anyone of my discovery that day. We lived in a big house, and, with twelve brothers and sisters, my things had a way of disappearing. I put the letter and the photograph in the small cedar box I kept hidden under my bed. Every so often I would read the letter and look at his photograph. One night I fell asleep before putting it away and only remembered it when I was at school. I knew my mother would find it and I worried she would take it away. When I came home the photograph was missing. I found it in the top drawer of my dresser, facedown.

I never left it out again.

Though I never knew my father, as a child I did know a few things about him. I knew that he had been a navy pilot and that he and my mother had met in the days just following the end of the Second World War. Before I was born, he and my mother and my four brothers had lived in Bermuda. At the time his plane went down, they had been married for ten years. Growing up, I was told that because no trace of his plane was ever found, he and his flight crew had disappeared in the Bermuda Triangle.

Finally, I knew that my mother was pregnant with me when he died. I never came out and directly asked my mother if my father had known she was pregnant. What if he hadn't? So this was the sum of what I knew and didn't know. I spent much of my childhood wanting to know more.

My fantasies about my father were easily nurtured by the silence that surrounded his death. The mystical aspect of the Bermuda Triangle fueled my imagination. I pictured him alive and living in the underwater city of Atlantis with the other pilots and crewmen aboard ships and planes that had mysteriously vanished without a trace. In another scenario I saw him sucked up into the universe. Untethered to Earth and its gravitational forces, his plane had shot into the sky through one of the black holes I was always hearing about.

When Charles Berlitz's *Bermuda Triangle* was published in 1975, I bought a copy and read it eagerly but was disappointed when I didn't find my father's name. Two years later Berlitz followed up with

5

Without a Trace, where I did find him mentioned. In a table listing planes and ships that had vanished in the Bermuda Triangle, I read that on November 9, 1956, a P5M with a crew of ten had disappeared 300 miles south of Bermuda. This bit of information, which seemed so factual, gave me solid proof of exactly where my father was on that day in November. Somehow it was comforting. It was as close as I had ever come to knowing where he died.

Like many children who have never known their fathers, I created one, and he was perfect. He was funny and he laughed a lot. I used to imagine him walking me home from school, helping me pull up my socks when they slipped into my sneakers. He loved to watch me run and play softball. My father was the one person in the world who would never hurt me, never reject me. I pictured him bursting with pride at my achievements, great and small, real and imagined. The fact that he was gone did not mean he did not exist and certainly did not keep me from thinking about him.

My mother moved back to California to be with her family within weeks of receiving the news of my father's death. When I was four, she married a widower with seven children; a few years later they had a child together, making us a family of fifteen. Since I couldn't have two fathers, I was told to call my new father Daddy and my real father Jack. My mother took very seriously the idea of making a new life for herself and her children. We all knew other navy widows in town who seemed never to have moved on, never to have gotten over the loss of their husbands. My mother didn't want to be like them.

As I grew older I tried to get my mother to tell me about my father. She did not talk easily about the past, but I knew some of the memories were happy ones, and I liked seeing her remember those times. For instance, she liked that their house in Bermuda was called "Mimosa Cottage." When she was relaxed and working in the garden, I could ask her questions. She told me he had planned to retire early from the military and write, that his aspiration to become a sportswriter had been put on hold when he entered the Naval Academy in 1939. He had hoped, she said, with some good investments, to buy a small-town newspaper. They had talked of living in the north county of San Diego, close to the racetrack in Del Mar, so my father could bet on the horses.

Coronado is home to many military families. When I was a child, every year at Christmas, the children whose fathers had died in active service would attend a party at the naval base's movie theater. They called us war orphans. Why was I a war orphan? I wondered. I certainly didn't consider myself an orphan — I had a mother and a man I called Daddy (or sir). My father's plane had merely disappeared on what I had been told was a simple milk run to Pensacola or Norfolk. He hadn't been killed in Vietnam or the Korean War or World War II. Yet we would be invited up onstage one at a time in alphabetical order and given a plastic red net stocking filled with candy. We would also get a present, and, as I remember, it was something impressive — like a bicycle. But even the prospect of getting a bicycle did not make getting on that stage any easier. None of us liked being in that room full of fatherless kids.

Because we were never told what actually happened, a veil of mystery seemed to hang about our lost fathers. You knew something had gone wrong somehow; they were gone and we were left behind. There was a kind of shame in it. We knew it wasn't supposed to be that way, but it was. When the Vietnam POWs were returning home in the early '70s several of my friends met fathers they didn't remember. Like me, they had grown up not knowing whether their fathers were alive or dead. Now they were meeting them. I clung a little to the hope that with the returning POWs my father would also return.

I remember once sitting on the beach in Coronado when I was about eleven with my best friend, Chris. He pointed across the ocean to a peninsula called Point Loma and said, "That's where my father is." I knew he meant the military cemetery located there. He asked me where my father was. Where was he? A father I'd never met in an ocean I'd never seen. I just mumbled, "Out there, too."

My mother only began to talk to me about my father when I was in my early twenties. I am sure she must have wanted to share him with me. One day beside the fig tree in our backyard that had been planted the day she was born, my mother described how she felt the March day I was born. Her hospital room was filled with flowers, and a nurse came in and exclaimed, "What beautiful flowers! Your husband must love you very much." She wept that day for the first time since receiving the news of my father's disappearance in November. Until I was born, she said, she focused on the tasks before her: packing up the family's belongings in Bermuda, closing the house and bank account, moving back to Coronado, settling the boys in school, and finding a new home.

Another time I asked her to tell me something about my father she didn't like. She thought about it awhile and said, "Everything he wore had to be ironed." "That's it?" I said. She nodded.

I remember being home from college on vacation once, lying on her bed and crying over my boyfriend, whom I missed terribly. My mother sat beside me, looking as pained as I felt. She didn't say anything except, "Oh sweetie, I'm so sorry." I thought, what could this middle-aged woman with thirteen children know about love? And suddenly it hit me. She had lost her husband, the love of her life, the father of her four sons, the father to her unborn daughter. I've never forgotten the look on her face that day.

While few people are prepared to deal with the kind of loss my mother suffered, she seemed particularly ill equipped to survive as a widow and the mother of five young children. Her childhood had been a charmed and sheltered one. Her father, nicknamed "Mr. Coronado" because of his dedicated civic service, was a local merchant. Her grandfather, who arrived in Coronado in 1887, when it was mostly sand, sagebrush, and Mexican cactus, opened its first post office in his general store. Her phone number was 1. Coronado itself — called "the enchanted island" — must have seemed at the time like an unreal place, a place where fairy tales are born and dreams come true. The Hotel del Coronado, which opened the year after my great-grandfather arrived, looks like the topping on a wedding cake, with its Victorian trelliswork and many gables. Like everyone else at that time, my mother believed that Thomas Edison himself installed the lights at the hotel, that Wallis Simpson met the Duke of Windsor there, and that Frank Baum was inspired to write *The Wizard of Oz* there. I've since learned these stories are just fanciful myths built around some small kernels of truth.

My mother and I often used to rummage together in the bottom drawer of her dresser. It was where she saved everything: heirloom jewelry, the ID bracelets her babies had worn in the hospital, family photographs, letters home from camp, report cards, that sort of thing. (She also saved plenty of unimportant things as well, like my driver's ed certificate and a partially filled-out application for the game show *Password*.) Once in a while she hid candy bars in there for me. Through the years she would explain the significance or history of a particular piece of jewelry that had belonged to her mother or father. Not long before she died we were looking through the drawer and she showed me a black-and-white photograph of her mother. On the back were the words "Mother in front of her favorite rose." I thought I was familiar with everything in that drawer.

In 1985 my mother died after a long struggle with

heart disease. On the morning following her funeral service I discovered toward the back of that dresser drawer a bundle of letters I'd never seen before. Held together by a faded pink ribbon, the bundle looked like it had not been opened in many years.

I know she left those letters there for me.

The letters remained tied up with their pink ribbon for a year after I found them. Finally, one morning I sat down with the bundle and opened the first envelope. I unfolded the stiff sheaf of pages and met my father at last.

was in love with you. It expla[ins]
[o]f queer things that have been p[uzz]
[fo]r instance, why I write you [so]
[l]etters, why I think about you [all]
[t]he day and dream about you mo[st]
[th]e night, and why I'm so eager [to]
[ba]ck to the _____ your fe[w]
[in]tuition _____ _____ so go[od]
[re]ce) you _____ it all
[th]ough. A _____ _____ at lo[ng]
[m]e for _____ any
[w]hich is _____ you[r]
[n]ow I'll never forget _____ thing ab[out]
[th]ose twelve days between Dec. 29
[Ja]n. 9 (Check?) Only two months ag[o]
[it] was that we were in the _____
[b]owl, the Biltmore Bowl, and, a d[ay]
[late]r, the Boysenberry Bowl.
     The amazing thing about it is
[strin]g of coincidences that set up t[he]

Lt. J. M. Sweeney USN
VH-1, % F.P.O.
San Francisco, Cal.

VIA AIR MAIL
UNITED STATES POSTAGE

Lt. J. M. Sweeney USN
VH-1, % F.P.O.
San Francisco, Cal.
air mail

U.S.
18
FEB
1946
NAVY

Miss Bebe Mathewson
1020 Park Place
Coronado, California

Part Two

Dear Beebe,

I didn't intend to run away without leaving you a little collateral with which to take care of my many financial problems which I left in your hands, but when I told you goodbye I guess my head was in the clouds so far that I couldn't give a thought to such earthly things as money. So I'm enclosing 30 skins (20 for the pictures, 2 or 3 for the laundry, and the rest for the Railway Express Co. unless you shipped the stuff collect, which is what I meant to tell you to do). If this isn't enough for the Ry. Exp., let me know. It's really sweet of you to take care of all my loose ends for me — as a matter of fact, I've been thinking the matter over and have come to the conclusion that meeting you was the luckiest break I've ever had in my somewhat lucky life.

This is our

(I just interrupted this literary effort to get into a small game of poker, in which I won $39.85 — sorry!)

17

This is our fourth day on the high seas, but it's the first letter I've gotten around to. Most of my time has been spent at the Acey-Ducey board with my friend Gill, who leads me 19 games to 14. (One dollar per game.) He won't play me any more gin rummy since I won 85 cents off him in an hour the first day.

We're due at Pearl Harbor Wednesday morning. How long I'll be there is anybody's guess.

Although I haven't written any letters before today, don't think I haven't had you on my mind ever since I saw you. I've thought of practically nothing else. (Maybe <u>that's</u> why Gill is beating me at Acey-Ducey.) It seems incredible to me that I could <u>miss</u> anyone so much that I've known for a couple of weeks, but I do. That last night was completely perfect. It already seems like a dream, and I'm sure I'll go over it again in my mind lots of times in the months to come. Now how about that letter? 'Sgo!

With much love,
and also a little fond affection,
Jack

Dearest Beebe,

Now writing at you from sunny Kaneohe (pronounced "Kaneohe"), Hawaii, which on a map (I always have a map) looks something like this way:

Speaking of maps, when are you going to send me a picture of 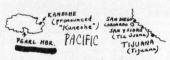 yours? Not that I don't retain in my photographic mind every detail of your lovely puss, but I may be away for some time and I don't wish to take any chances whatever on forgetting. Be sure that the picture includes that little top-knot I like so much. I don't suppose you could have it in technicolor so I could get the full effect of your eyes, could you?

We got here Wednesday, and Friday I went out to the good old Oahu Country Club for a few golfs. I played my usual game. At least the flowers out there smelled good. I certainly wish you were here — we could have a wonderful time doing lots of things, golfing, swimming at Waikiki, dancing, and stuff.

Before long I'll probably be wishing I were here too, because I'm leaving Tuesday for points west, and I do mean west. First stop is Okinawa, by way of Kwajalein and Guam. From there it may be Tokyo or Japan or somewhere like that.

I just had a happy thought — we will cross the international date line Wednesday, which is supposed to be my birthday, but then it will be Thursday instead of Wednesday on account of crossing the line, so I won't have a birthday and I'll get to be 25 another year instead of 26! How to keep from growing old.

The last thing you said to me was "I'll see you in a couple of months." You may have to keep saying that for many months, but I hope you will.

By the way — did Horatio show up after I left your house the other night? If he did, he's a persevering little cuss. The return address on the envelope will eventually reach me. You might try it for size.

Love,
Jack

Sunday, Jan 27

Dear Beebe,

Still eagerly awaiting that first letter from you, although I know it's a couple of weeks too early to really expect one. Mail service isn't so hot when you get out this far in the country.

I'm writing this from the seaplane tender <u>Curtiss,</u> which is anchored in the harbor of Okinawa. Sixteen of us arrived here today after flying all night from Guam, which is where I spent all day Saturday. We got our squadron assignments today, and I was a little disappointed in mine. They separated Gillock and me. He is an Academy classmate and we have been together all through flight training, for the past year and a half. But it had to come sooner or later.

I feel a lot better today for one reason, though — being on this ship gave me the opportunity to get cleaned up for the first time in several days. Ever since we left Kaneohe (pronounced "Kaneohe") life has been pretty rough — sleeping in quonset huts and eating lousy food — so today after a shower, shave, and a change to clean clothes I feel pretty good, even though the immediate future isn't so bright. Not enough of you in it.

Tuesday I'm flying to Shanghai, which I understand is over by China somewhere (I lost my map), to report to squadron headquarters. Then I hope I'll stay there long enough to let some mail catch up to me. Just to make sure you'd write me, I mailed you a little pikake-shell lei before leaving Hawaii so you'll have to write and thank me for that, see.

By the way, my present return address (VH-1) should be fairly permanent. Please feel free to use it any time you feel like it. I surely will be glad to hear from you — there's so many things I'd like to know, like what you've been doing, and did you get my golf bats checked in, and did my laundry ever come back, and did Horatio ever show up after I left, and how many children we're going to have after we're married, and if there's anything new on who knows what about Clyde and Aleon (how the heck do you spell that?) and if you came out as lucky in last Sunday afternoon's tea fight at the new, monstrous, sprawling Del Coronado as you did in the one previous; namely, with me.

Saturday night during our layover in Guam I sat out in the rain to see a USO play called "What a Life." (The original Henry Aldrich play.) Sounds like a silly thing to do, but about a thousand other supposedly intelligent servicemen did likewise and also enjoyed it.

I ran into Stewart, the officer who was in the Colony with his wife (or <u>somebody's</u> wife) that last night we were there, and he asked me who the gorgeous creature was that I was with. (I knew right off he meant you, dear.) That's the way I like to remember you best. I've never seen a more beautiful sight in my life than you sitting across that table in candlelight, surrounded by filet mignons and profiteroles. Why couldn't I have met you when you were young? Thirty-three* is a pretty advanced age, you must admit.

Love,
Jack

*She was, of course, twenty-three.

23

P.S. Am enclosing my horoscope for my birthday.
Looks like Stella's got me pegged, all right!

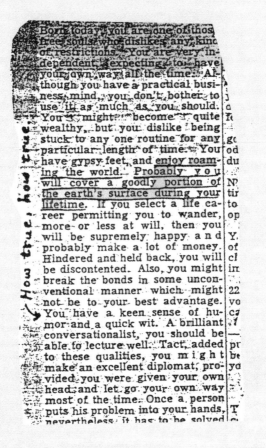

Dearest Beebe,

I don't understand why I'm writing you so often. I'm generally a pretty bad correspondent, and here I am writing you for about the fortieth time. Even if you only answer half of 'em, I'll still be getting more mail than usual.

I had a dream about you last night. You were beating a filet mignon to death with a golf club. I think it was a 7-iron. I didn't count how many strokes you took but I remember thinking you were way over par for the course. (Meat course, of course.) I've had better dreams of you than that one.

I saw a mess of LCT's anchored in a little bay yesterday and there was a sign pointing that way that said "To Elsie Teeville." Darned clever, these amphibious boys. By the way, how's Ed, the ace of the base? You don't know, I hope.

I'm getting to be a pretty sharp bridge player.

25

Today I even won playing with Gillock, who is just learning.

Tomorrow I'm off to Shanghai. Keep your eye on the funnies, because I'm liable to show up in Terry and the Pirates any day now.

Love,
Jack

P.S. You can send me those pictures any time now. The natives here are begging for them. I can get a glass of saki for 6 pictures.

Dearest Beebe,

Looks like I've finally settled down in one place for awhile, and this isn't a bad place to do it, except it's a little chilly. (If this was Japan I could get off a good one by saying it was nippy, but this isn't, so I can't.) Now if that old mail will start coming in, I might feel that it's not such a hard life after all.

I guess my eagerness to hear from you isn't any worse than that of another guy in my squadron who got a note from his mother-in-law while we were in Hawaii saying that his baby had just been born. But she didn't say whether it was a boy or a girl, and since we haven't had any mail since then, the poor guy doesn't know whether he's a father or a mother. So he's pretty anxious for some mail to catch up with us, too.

A couple of us went ashore the first night (we're living on a seaplane tender anchored in the Whangpoo River) and had a lot of fun spending Chinese money. China is so inflated that an American dollar can be exchanged for about 1,400 Chinese dollars. We had dinner at the officers' club, the bill coming to 3,800 dollars. You should've seen me nonchalantly tip the waiter 500 bucks.

The club was a nice-looking place — orchestra, dance floor, etc. And what do you think they're playing in Shanghai these days? "Just a Little Fond Affection"! It sure made me wish you were there.

I brought my little old radio with me and she's all hooked up and working like a charm. The Armed Forces Radio broadcasts transcriptions of all the good programs. We wouldn't even have the slightest chance for an argument here, because they don't have Fibber McGee and "This Is the Best I Can Do," or whatever that favorite of yours is called, at the same time.

I'm certainly glad I traveled light. I was the only one who didn't have to ship a big trunk back home from Hawaii, because they limited us to 100 lbs. baggage from there to here.

Well, adios, hasta luego cielito lindo y tia juana; which, in case you don't know Spanish and I hope you don't, means "Love & kisses,"

Jack

Dear Beebe,

Saturday night is the loneliest night in the week, all right. I'm writing this from my good old airplane, H-2, which is moored to a buoy in Tsingtao Harbor (pronounced "har'-ber). Contrary to my hopes and expectations, the mail did not catch up with me in Shanghai, and so I'm now looking forward to it up here.

Tsingtao is no Shanghai. In fact, I suspect the Navy of sending us to Tsingtao for a couple of weeks just so when we get back to Shanghai it will look so good to us we will forget to gripe about not being in Coronado.

Before I let myself go and wax romantical or something, it's a beautiful moonlight night tonight, and what I'm doing on this airplane is being on watch out here in case the plane breaks loose from the buoy. It's colder than the dickens, but when winter comes, can spring be far behind? Unquote. Tsingtao looks very picturesque from the air, being a little town built by the Germans long ago, but I went ashore the other day and it's really pretty dirty. The streets are full of dirty Chinese kids who are pretty funny to talk to but who are always trying to sell something. I bought you a little present. The kid wanted 6,000 Chinese dollars for it, but I traded him my 1943 yo-yo for it and he thinks he got to the best of me. Maybe he did, at that — the string on it was fairly new.

Although life in general is pretty dull for me right now, there's always a little sweet with the sour. We've been playing a quaint little Chinese game on the ship called "Po-Kerr," and in the week I've been here I have amassed the tidy sum of 250 good old American bucks, all clear profit. I don't care if I draw any pay or not, just so they let me keep playing.

'Sgo with that letter!

Love,
Jack

(over for P.S.)

P.S. The first <u>five</u> days of February are celebrated here in China as New Year's. Somebody asked me if I didn't think it was peculiar, using several days to celebrate New Year's and I said no, I had tried it myself and thought it was a wonderful idea.

P.P.S. Another thing I've wondered about is whether I'm sending your letters to the right address. You probably have a box number in the post office which I should use. Maybe I'll know, one of these days.

P.P.P.S. Tell Glen Ellen and Nancy hello for me. And you know what you can tell Ed Jones and Horatio for me. On second thought, you'd better not, as I don't like for you to use that kind of language.

Tsingtao,
Saturday, Feb. 23

Hello, honey —

MAIL!!! Today it happened! Only 45 days since I told you goodbye, a little bundle of letters for me comes in, and right there on the bottom was the one I was praying for — from Coronado, Cal, postmarked Feb. 6.

Well, I immediately rips it open and out falls a newspaper clipping. I just get a glimpse of some headlines about "Miss M — (some long name beginning with M) Recites Vows in Sausalito." When I come to, there is somebody fanning me and saying "Give him air, give him air!" I say "Never mind — just let me die, please. Women are a snare and a delusion and life is not worth living."

Of course later I find out it is a Miss Marxmiller who does the reciting and not Miss Mathewson, but I consider this very unkind of you to throw something like that in your very first letter to me with no warning. It could easily have been fatal.

Otherwise this letter of yours was the biggest thing that's happened in my life since I left the USA. Frankly it tickled me to death. You write just like you talk, and reading your letter brought back sweet memories of me driving the old Blue Blunder Bus with you babbling along merrily at my side, and there's nobody I'd rather be babbling with than you.

I wish I'd known you were going to New Orleans sooner, because I don't think this letter will reach you in time to give you the dope. I hope you visited the Blue Room in the Roosevelt, had shrimp at Arnaud's (that reminds me — how's Horatio?), dined at the Court of the Two Sisters, and didn't flirt with the naval officers who overrun the town.

I wonder how long your commendable abstinence from alcoholic beverages lasted, my deah. Wouldn't it be peachy if we both vowed we wouldn't down another Old Fashioned until we did it together, only you probably wouldn't last and neither would I. As a matter of fact, though, I've been remarkably pure myself since going west. Except for a few beers in Hawaii and a few vodkas in Shanghai, I haven't indulged. Every time I start to drink I think of you saying "'Sgo'" and I get sorta homesick or something. I may as well admit it — I'm deeply in love with you, Beebe, and that's no kiddin'. Sorry to break up our beautiful friendship, but that's how it is.

Now to go from the sublime to the ridiculous, my pictures will probably arrive in time for me to chuckle over them in my old age. That's probably the worst $30 I ever spent — when I ordered them I thought I had dozens of people to send them to, but now that you've got your copy, I don't know what to do with the rest. Oh well, I have lots of sisters and they'll (the pictures) solve my Christmas shopping problem next year, or the year after.

I can hardly wait to get your picture. I'm beginning to be afraid that the mental picture of you which I carry around is getting exaggerated. You're beautiful, all right, but you <u>can't</u> be as luscious as I remember you. I need a picture to serve as a sort of anchor on my imagination, see.

Also I can hardly wait for those sox. You couldn't

have selected a more appropriate gift — I'm freezing to death right this minute, and I think my tootsies are getting the worst of it. I know I'm lucky to be getting a pair of such expertly-made socks, he replied gallantly through chattering teeth.

You probably won't get this till you're back from your Florida jaunt so I'll say I hope you had a good time except for missing me so much. By the way — is the Peggy you're going with the same one I smacked New Year's Eve? If so, regards to her & congratulations to her husband. And love to you, sweetie.

Jack

Dearest Beeb,

After reading your letter over for the sixteenth time and doing a little reminiscing on my own hook, I've come across a terrible error in your letter which proves beyond a doubt that you have forgotten me already. You wrote the letter on Feb. 4 and said, quote, a month ago tonight we were at the Troc. Now I'll be willing to wager our usual nickel that on Jan. 4 we did nothing but go to the movies ("Leave Her to Heaven" with Gene Tierney and Paul Muni) and on the way home we had a chocolate sundae (apiece) at the Colony. You don't remember, and I could just cry. I think I <u>will</u> cry. Boo hoo hoo, you brute, you.

You didn't say how long you'd be in Florida. Maybe you didn't know yet. By the way, if the Southern California C. of C. hears that you've gone to Florida for the winter, heaven help you when you get back. I'll bet you have a lot of fun on that trip,

36

though. I wish I were with you. If you get any snap-shots while in Florida, have an extra one taken for me. In bathing suit, natch. Have you ever been pinned up before? <u>Since</u> infancy, silly.

One of the other letters I got yesterday was from my little sister who is in dramatic school in New York, and it was almost as hilarious as yours. If you remember, <u>which I doubt</u>, I told you she was appear-ing in her first real New York play, "Hay Fever," about the time I left San Diego, and in her review of the show she says, with typical Sweeney modesty, "Everyone says I was the best one in it. I brought down the house twice and got applause on every exit." She graduates March 15. Hollywood, the line forms just outside Miss Sweeney's dressing room.

A couple of days ago VH-1 got a call from a sink-ing Chinese ship. So we dash out over the Yellow Sea and are we surprised when we find it! It was almost gone when our plane spotted it, but we dropped some life rafts and all but two of them were picked up by a destroyer later in the day. Never a dull moment in VH-1. Do you know what a PBM looks like yet?

Tsingtao, March 1

Dearest Beebe,

I'm certainly glad I figured out that I was in love with you. It explains a lot of queer things that have been puzzling me — for instance, why I write you so many letters, why I think about you most of the day and dream about you most of the night, and why I'm so eager to get back to the states. With your female intuition (which doesn't work so good on horses) you probably knew it all along, though. And even if this great love I have for you never does me any good (which is up to nobody but you), I know I'll never forget anything about those twelve days between Dec. 29 and Jan. 9. (Check?) Only two months ago today it was that we were in the Rose Bowl, the Biltmore Bowl, and, a day later, the Boysenberry Bowl.

The amazing thing about it is the string of coincidences that set up the whole thing. I think it was the

27th of December that I was all set to drive up to San Francisco with my friend Danny. To be perfectly frank, I was on my way up there to see a girl I knew. But I had a strange feeling for some reason that I wouldn't have a good time up there — why, I don't know, because at that time, I had no reason to think I'd have a better one in San Diego. I'm not the kind of guy who goes around doing whatever "strange feelings" tell me to do, but I know I felt a lot better after I told Danny I'd decided not to go — about two hours before he left. If I'd gone, of course, you'd still be nothing to me but that good-looking blonde at the Squadron Party whom I wish I'd known better.

And then if Nancy hadn't already had a date for New Year's Eve — you knew you were second choice, of course, the last time you ever will be second choice for me. If Nancy hadn't suggested you as an alternate, I'd have tried you anyhow, because I'd been thinking about you in a hopeless sort of way ever since meeting you at the Squadron Party.

What gets my goat is that I was back there in the states for a whole year and a half (June '44 to Jan. '46) and I have to wait till twelve days before I go to China before meeting the girl of my dreams. Doesn't that take the rag off'n the bush?

I'm anxious to hear about that sensational cross-country tour of yours, which starts tomorrow according to my info. In fact, I'm anxious to hear anything from you. I've still received only that one little batch of mail containing that one letter of Feb 4–5 from you. I've just about got that one memorized by now and am ready for fresh reading material. We're going back to Shanghai in a few days, and I hope to find a couple from you waiting for me there.

You asked me what Shanghai was like. Well, as the geography books say, it's a curious mixture of the ancient East and the modern West. There are lots of tall, modern office buildings and hotels, but the streets are full of rickshaws and open-air shops where you have to bargain for what you want to buy, like in Mexico and South America, only the Chinese seem to be more friendly and politer about the bargaining than the Latin Americans. You know the old saying about the East is East and West is West and never the twain shall meet. I haven't had to meet any twains, myself, but I rode on one of the twolley cars. Brother!

I hope you took your stationery and fountain pen along with you to Florida and write me a letter or two while you're basking in the sun. Or at least drop me a little old postcard from New Orleans or somewhere. Or at least just think about me once or twice.

All my love,
Jack

And remember!
L.S. — M.F.T.
(Let's Stayhome — Molly & Fibber Tonight!)

air mail

Dear Beatrice,

Well, whaddayuh know — another letter from my big moment comes in today, with a side dish of Valentines. In reply to the latter, you're darn tootin' I'll be your Valentine. In reply to the letter, quote:

Say, honeybunch, what is this Marie business you keep giving me? Don't tell me they've finally located that Russian who gave your mother a bad time back in 1912 (1946 minus 34 = '12*) and they've found out your name isn't Beebe after all, it's Marie on your father's side. You've got me even more confused than usual, with that Marie stuff. After all, don't you think I deserve to at least know the real name of

---

He's teasing her again about her age. She wasn't thirty-four years old.

43

who I'm in love with? If I don't receive a satisfactory reply to this simple question within two months, I'm going to start calling you Ann, as I've always wanted to know a girl name of Ann. (I think Marie is also pretty.) (Just in case.)

I have decided that the little number down in the corner of the envelope is to let me know how many letters you've written me. In that case I haven't received No. 1 yet, but I have 2 and 3. Maybe No. 1 explains about Marie?

I suppose you're somewhere between Coronado and Florida right now. If I could've gotten a letter to you before you left, I'd've given you complete instructions on how to find the Sweeney domicile, as it is only about three blocks off the highway between Coronado and Florida, and you could stop there to water the horses and take on supplies and provisions and rest in the shade of the old apple tree and meet my fine father and mother and any other Sweeneys who may be still hanging around the old homestead. No kidding, Beebe, there's nothing would please me more than for you to stop off there, for after meeting

I haven't seen but one good movie since I left, and it was "Wonder Man" — for the third time. But I hear all kinds of good radio programs. And no commercials. Not even Kelly can penetrate the sanctity of the Armed Forces Radio Service. All the programs are about three months behind the ones in the states, though, as they are just recordings of the actual broadcasts and it takes a long time to get 'em around to all the overseas radio stations. I've heard several programs out here that I heard while I was in San Diego.

Almost every song I hear reminds me of somewhere that you and I have been together. For instance, "Melancholy Baby" takes me back to the Marine Room; "Don't Blame Me" is New Year's Eve at Camp Kidd (why, I don't know — I don't remember them playing it but once); "Just a Little Fond Affection" fits in almost anywhere — Camp Kidd, the Biltmore Bowl, the slot machine in Lowrey Annex Bar, or sitting in my car out in front of your house. I <u>could</u> say "All or Nothing at All" reminds me of your fabulous ham-and-egg-and-cheese-and-bacon-and-lettuce-and-tomato sandwich (toasted), but I won't.

My latest book, "How to Play Winning Gin Rummy," hits the newsstands this week.

I love you,
Jack

P.S. What do you mean saying we have known each other only a short time? We've known each other two years — 1945 and 1946.

Tsingtao, China,
Sunday, March 10

Dearest Beatrice Marie Bernadette
Jennifer Beebe, honeychile,

Just got back from Shanghai after a two-day visit. Asked the boys at squadron headquarters where all my mail was and they said they'd just sent it up to Tsingtao the day before. On arrival back here, I found it all piled up on my desk — one single solitary letter, of Feb. 14 vintage — but it was from you (No. 4 — still no No. 1), so I'm not complaining at all.

I'm so proud of you for working that whole day as a real live secretary. Is there no limit to your versatility? Red Crosser, knitter, cook, golfer, and now secretary! (Did I leave out anything?)

If you have any more dreams as crazy as the one about me being in Coronado without calling you, you better see a doctor.

I had a pretty good time in Shanghai — nothing spectacular. There are quite a few American and

48

Russian girls there, but I just didn't have the yen for them. (No pun intended, really.) I find myself continually comparing every girl I see with you. They invariably come out second best. I think you spoiled me — nobody else seems to be good enough for me any more. How long does this go on?

I am still flying as a co-pilot with Buck. They say they're going to check me out as a P.P.C. [Patrol Plane Commander] soon, with a plane and crew of my own, although I've had little PBM [Patrol Bomber Mariner] experience compared with other P.P.C.'s.

I suppose you're sunning yourself in Florida right now. I haven't even seen the sun in weeks. The stars did come out the other night, though, and I saw Mars and Saturn up there and thought of the night we went out to the Marine Room and the Trocadero and almost rode the ferris wheel. I wonder if you can still pick out Mars and Saturn. It seems impossible when I figure up what time it is where you are and find out that when the sun is overhead here, the stars are still out for the night before in Florida.

Everyone out here is disgusted with the way the

mail is handled. Some organization in Tokyo demanded a Congressional investigation the other day, I read. There really is no excuse for that first letter of yours not reaching me before now — you didn't start with No. 2, did you?

Seriously, Beebe, you're really being sweet to me with your letters — I look forward to them more than I can tell you.

All my love,
Jack

P.S. How come the last letter wasn't SWAK? Is rationing on again?

SWABOGK

Ding how, my little lotus bud,

(Eng. Translation: hiya, toots)

I'm freezing to death so thought I'd sit down and write you a few — just thinking about you warms me up.

I just got back to my room after seeing another sorry movie. There was a peachy cartoon, though — a "Goofy" called "Hockey Homicide." Don't miss it — I laughed so hard I hurt all over and had to shut my eyes so I could catch my breath. The other night the ship had "Wonder Man." Having nothing else to do, I took it in for the fourth time. Danny Kaye gets the girl at the end every time.

This morning was rough. I spent the night on duty out in the plane and when we got up this morning we found the port float under water, which is several feet lower than normal. So we spent all morning pumping water out of it — it seems somebody forgot to put the inspection cover back on tight, and it came off during the night. Lucky we didn't sink. And was it cold out there!

Where, oh where are those socks? After all, it's only ten months till my birthday, and I fear they won't arrive in time.

Made 28 bucks in a game of Black Jack last night. And they pay me a salary, too!

Haven't received any mail recently. I can hardly wait for the reports on the Florida trip, although I probably won't hear about it till next month some time. I certainly hope you stop off in my home town on the way back, but you're probably coming back on the train and won't get a chance.

I keep hearing rumors that the squadron is pulling out of China soon. I wish we were heading for San Diego myself, but I guess that's just a dream for awhile yet. Nice dream, though — I practice on it every night. And you're right in the middle of it every time, Beebe.

Love & smooches,
Jack

TSINGTAO, CHINA,

MARCH 16, 1946

ONLY 5 MORE DAYS TILL SPRING

DEAREST BEEBE,

I AM WRITING THIS FROM MY AIRPLANE WHICH IS MOORED (I HOPE) TO A BUOY IN THIS HARBOR WHICH IS REALLY NOTHING BETTER THAN THE OPEN SEA BECAUSE THE WIND IS BLOWING LIKE EVERYTHING AND THE WAVES ARE LIKE MOUNTAINS AND THE PLANE IS GOING UP AND DOWN AND UP AND DOWN AND UP AND DOWN AND IT IS A VERY GOOD THING I DO NOT GET SEASICK, AS THERE IS NO TELLING WHEN THEY WILL BE ABLE TO GET A BOAT OUT HERE TO RELIEVE US. WE (ME AND THE THREE ENLIST-ED MEN WHO HAVE THIS WATCH WITH ME) WERE SUPPOSED TO BE RELIEVED THIS MORNING SEE BUT IT IS TOO STORMY TO GET A BOAT TO US SO HERE WE ARE AS YOU MIGHT SAY. THIS TRIPEWRITER IS THE ONE WHICH WE USE ON THE PLANE TO TAKE DOWN RADIO MESSAGES ON AND SEEMS TO HAVE NOTHING ON IT BUT CAPITAL LETTERS.

MY BIG NEWS FLASH TODAY IS THAT MY SQUADRON IS MOVING TO SAIPAN AS SOON AS THE WEATHER PERMITS. IN CASE YOU DON'T HAVE A MAP HANDY (YOU SHOULD ALWAYS HAVE A MAP HANDY) I'LL EXPLAIN THAT SAIPAN IS IN THE SAME GROUP OF ISLANDS WITH GUAM, ONLY ABOUT 120 MILES NORTH. IN A WAY IT'LL BE A WELCOME CHANGE. IT'LL BE WARM THERE AND WE'LL LIVE ASHORE WHERE WE'LL BE ABLE TO PLAY TENNIS AND BASEBALL AND SWIM A LITTLE. I NEED THE EXERCISE; I HAVEN'T HAD ANY TO SPEAK OF, BEYOND FIGHTING OFF LIT-TLE CHINESE URCHINS WHO TRY TO SELL ME SOME SILLY LITTLE KNICKNACK AND NEARLY ALWAYS SUCCEED. I'VE HAD SO LITTLE EXERCISE I'M BEGINNING TO GET THAT WELL-KNOWN TIRE AROUND MY WAISTLINE; IF I DON'T START WORKING IT OFF SOON WE'LL HAVE TO DANCE SIDESADDLE WHEN I COME BACK.

THIS PLANE WATCH GETS TO BE A LITTLE TIRESOME WHEN IT STRETCHES INTO TWO DAYS LIKE THIS. AT LEAST WE HAVE THE OLD RADIO TO LISTEN TO. NOTHING BUT GOOD PROGRAMS

ALL DAY LONG — LAST NIGHT, FOR INSTANCE, THEY HAD A HILARIOUS ONE WITH FIBBER MCGEE AND MOLLY IN IT. THEY ALWAYS BROAD-CAST THE BEST PROGRAMS AGAIN THE FOLLOW-ING MORNING FOR THOSE WHO MIGHT HAVE MISSED THEM THE NIGHT BEFORE, AND THIS MORNING I LISTENED TO THEM AGAIN TO CATCH THE PARTS I MISSED LAST NIGHT FROM LAUGHING SO HARD. THEY'RE DYNAMITE, SHEER DYNAMITE.

AS YOU NOTICE, I'M STILL ADDRESSING YOUR LETTERS TO BEEBE MATHEWSON TILL I HEAR SOMETHING DEFINITE ABOUT THIS MARIE BUSI-NESS. ALL I HAVE SO FAR IS CIRCUMSTANTIAL EVIDENCE SUCH AS YOU PUT ON THE BACK OF YOUR ENVELOPES, AND AFTER ALL YOU CAN'T EXPECT ME TO SUDDENLY START WRITING "DEAREST MARIE" OR "MARIE, MY DARLING" WHEN I DIDN'T EVEN KNOW I KNEW ANYBODY NAMED MARIE. BY THE WAY, ARE YOU KIN TO CHRISTY MATHEWSON? HE WAS A FAMOUS OLD PITCHER FOR THE NEW YORK GIANTS WHO ALSO HAD SOME NICE CURVES.

March 28, 1946

Hello, gorgeous,

There has been a slight pause for station identification. Having identified my station, I am free to announce that I'm now writing at you from that pearl of the Pacific known as Saipan. (Just north of Guam. You know where Guam is, I know.) When I got here, there were two letters from you waiting for me, which always makes things peachy. The most recent one was Mar. 4 and was your first position report on this fabulous trip through Texas (long may she wave), Florida, New York, and intermediate pts. (That stands for points, not pints, I hope.) I'd give anything to be on a trip like that with you, Beebe — I bet you screwballs were really having a big time. As a matter of fact, I can't imagine doing <u>anything</u> with you and not having a big time, so there!

Speaking of love, I love Saipan also. No kiddin', this is a welcome change from China in lots of ways.

Nice sunny weather, lots of facilities for sports of various kinds, and the squadron is all together here instead of being spread out as we were in Shangahi, Tsingtao, and Okinawa. Speaking of sports, your modest hero is the squadron athletic officer, pitcher on the softball team, and one of the sharpest horseshoe pitchers you'll ever see. I also made a stab at playing basketball Sunday and it nearly killed me. I'm not quite in the pink yet, see.

Besides, it was quite a thrill for me to return to Saipan, where only two years ago this June I practically single-handedly annihilated 20,000 Japs while serving aboard the USS Tennessee. I must tell you about it some time. I always figured I'd tell my grandchildren about it some day, but maybe I can rope you in on the same lecture.

And here's some jolly news — our squadron is scheduled for being decommissioned, which means going p-f-f-f-t all of a sudden, with all hands reporting to the states for redistribution, I hope. All of which means I have an excellent chance of seeing you again within a few months. So keep the candle burning in the window — we may make the Rose Bowl again next year!

The pictures and sox still haven't arrived. Now that I'm not cold any longer, that picture of you is my primary desire. In Tsingtao, I'll have to admit I was looking for those expertly-knitted sox almost as eagerly as for the picture of you, which <u>may</u> prove that a man's heart is in his big toe instead of his stomach as was formerly thought. But either one will be plenty welcome. In fact, I'll settle for a postcard from Texas, if it has a picture on the front.

A bunch of us toured the island in a jeep Sunday afternoon and wound up at a party at the club where there were 35 officers and three U.S.O. show girls. I actually danced one time with one of the critters — just to keep in practice for you, natch.

Well, it's getting late (9:30) so I'd better start thinking about kissing you good night, Beebe. Sweet dreams yourself.

All my love,
Jack.

P.S. Do you believe in large families?

P.P.S. Still have never received your No. 1 letter. It <u>must</u> have the word on this "Marie" thing. Can it possibly be that Beebe is just a nickname, I ask myself? What I want to know is — is you is or is you ain't my Beebe?

April 5, 1946

Dearest Beebe,

Ah, spring is here once again, and in the spring a young man's fancy lightly turns to thoughts of you, as if he hadn't been thinking of you constantly all winter.

I got your communiqué from St. Augustine yesterday — the sample-sized one with the picture on the back. Which is like giving a man a tea-cake when he's looking for a filet mignon and french fries and a profiterole. But I'm not complaining.

I take it you've completely devastated New York and the rest of the eastern U.S. by now and are back in Coronado. I certainly hope I'm on your circulation list when you start dishing out the reports on what you did to New York and vice versa. If you'd told me earlier that you were going to hit the big city on this scandalous voyage of yours, I'd've made you look up my little (19 yrs.) sister Julia who was just finishing her dramatic school at that time. She is just as blond as you and almost as cute. But undoubtedly your New York stay was full enough as it was so it's just as well.

There's no more word on what I wrote you before about decommissioning VH-1 back to the states. I'm actually hoping it won't be for about three more months — not because I like Saipan all that much, but because if it happens any sooner than that, old Sweeney is apt to find himself shunted off to some other squadron out here on account of having left San Diego such a short time ago. (Yes, honey, <u>you</u> and <u>I</u> know it was a million years ago, but the Navy uses a nasty old calendar, see.)

They do have a nice officers' club here, probably one of the better island clubs and the price list runs like this: Coca-colas, 10¢; beer, 10¢; all mixed drinks, 10¢. It's a good thing I don't drink much. Hic! Excuse me. But really I don't.

About all we've been doing the past few weeks is dodging the weather. We got word a typhoon was on its way last Thursday and rumor was rampant as to where we would evacuate to. Places from Hong Kong and Tokyo were mentioned, with me holding out for North Island down to the bitter end. We finally compromised by going back to Okinawa and spent three pleasant days there on a seaplane tender. The first day I was there we played a little poker with a limit of 25¢ on, and I lost 17 bucks. The next two days I got in with a bunch of the boys who like to play with no limit and I won 45 one day and 35 the next, and finished off the trip that night at the club by winning 24 at Black Jack. Can one be lucky at cards and love at the same time, I hope? How this old green stuff does keep piling up on me!

My radio lay down and died on me a couple of days ago, despite my sitting up by it and nursing it night after night. So yesterday I went up to the Army P.X. disguised as a dogface and bought a new radio for $55. It's probably not worth five, but at the rate I play poker I can afford it. Besides, I've got to have Fibber McGee and Molly, at any price.

I was talking about the weather, though. We got back from Okinawa Tuesday just in time to flee to the

Dearest Beebe,

At last I got No. 8 out of you! I don't know where No. 7 went, unless it's that postcard from St. Augustine. I still haven't seen No. 1. I was about to go nuts waiting out No. 8, but it was such a nice long one and such a good report on your trip that I'll have to forgive you just this once. BUT DON'T DO IT AGAIN!!!

It was quite a surprise, about Glen and Harry. Just goes to show, you never can tell. He's a lucky boy. Ordinarily I'd say they didn't know each other long enough to be marrying up like that, but those two weeks I knew you changed my mind on how long people should know each other to — well, to know each other. I guess it just depends on what kind of people they are, whether people should know each other longer or not. Confused, aren't you? Glad to know you, Confused; I'm Jack — I mean John. Which reminds me, old garter belt, what is <u>your</u> name? About calling me John, permission is hereby granted. In fact, you can call me Horatio or Ed or anything like that, just so you call <u>me</u>. I think horoscopes are peachy, Cahuenga, — in fact, I wouldn't dream of going anywhere without mine on — but just what the heck has calling me John got to do with horoscopes? You are undoubtedly the craziest female woman I've ever been in love with.

Now for the criticism on your Report of Travels. Naturally my feelings are somewhat injured over your remarks about my native land, although I must admit there is some truth in them. Too bad you went through the wrong part of the state — that's like somebody traveling through California's deserts without ever seeing San Francisco, Los Angeles, or <u>Coronado</u> and then saying they didn't think much of California.

Take my home, for instance — we have a big grassy lawn and grapevine all over the front porch and several big peach trees scattered around and stuff like that. Honest, Texas isn't <u>all</u> sand!

Speaking of states, where is this one name of Complete Exhaustion that you said you were going to end your trip in?

Life on Saipan has settled into some sort of routine after the first hectic days during which we were running all over the island in a jeep and finding out what officers' clubs we would be welcome in and could go to have a good time if the occasion ever arose, and which ones we would be kicked out of. Lately I haven't been straying from the base, though; my work as Squadron Personnel Officer and Air-Sea Rescue Officer of the Saipan area keep me fairly busy during the day and at night I generally go to the movies or listen to the radio.

This really is a beautiful island — it gets a little warm during the day but the evenings are nice and cool. If you'd get back in the Red Cross and get them to send you out here to serve me coffee and doughnuts and things I wouldn't mind this island at all. They don't even have any Red Crossers on Saipan, though.

Still have no picture, no sox.

All my love,
Jack.

P.S. SWABOGK means "Sealed With A Big Ole Gooey Kiss." The kind that make you say "My, My!"

Thursday, April 25

Ann, darlin',

Got two at once this time — nice going. I'll send you the measurements on the sweater in my next letter. I am highly flabbergasted and extremely bumfuzzled to think that I am really going to get one of those expertly-made sweaters. Or have you stopped knitting?

I got a big kick out of reading about your trip about the countryside, only I wish it had been me there to show it to you. Only thing is, you didn't tell me anything about your various romances along the way, which I'm sure must have been numerous as I have personally seen you in action at tea parties picking up poor defenseless naval officers like mad when all they dropped in for was a cup of tea. So come on, Blondie, give up some lurid details — meet any prospective third husbands?

Your request to be my Easter bunny arrived two days late, but I had you in mind for the job all along.

But don't forget the old saying — hare today and gone tomorrow. Merry Christmas and Happy Easter Egg!

Which reminds me — how do you like this song about "It was just a New Year's Eve dance — That's all that it was — But oh, what it seemed to be." Frankie sings it, almost. Or "That's not ants in the sugar, Mother — you're putting your dice in the tea."

On dogs and cats, now, I'm afraid we can't get up much of an argument. But "Fibber McGee & Molly" forever. I like some dogs and I like some cats. I can't give you a definite quote on either one — I had a dog once name of Bozo whom I was very fond of and vice versa, but then I also knew a cat once name of Topaz who was a very steady individual even though female. I also knew one named Marie who was nice (female — not cat). There I go getting off the subject again.

That <u>was</u> sorta nasty of me to leave China before your sox arrived. (I always have to write that "sox" carefully so it won't look like "sex." <u>You'd</u> know what I meant, but how about the people who'll read this forty years from now in "Famous Letters of Famous Naval Heroes" compiled by Lt. J. M. Sweeney, USN (Retired)?)

By the way, did you read about Congress raising my salary? Darn decent of the chaps, although it isn't as if I had done nothing to deserve it. Of course the Senate still has to pass the bill, but — a mere formality, dear.

You're asking for another picture of me and I haven't even got the first one of you yet. Such is the price we celebrities must pay. The only picture I have of you is in my memory, but I don't think it'll wear off. Seriously, Cotton, I miss you more all the time. I thought <u>possibly</u> when I first left you, way back there in January, that the reason I thought of nothing but you was that it was the most recent happening in my life; but the longer I'm away, the better perspective I seem to get and the more I realize that you're the most wonderful girl I've known.

Write back quick like a fox.

Lurve,
Jack

Note: Jack added in the left margin of the second page: EDITOR'S NOTE — THIS PAGE GOT RAINED ON. SORRY.

*Wednesday, Apr 30**

Hello, Swede heart,

Did I make a haul today! Your sox and picture arrived today, right alongside of Letter No. 14 (what happened to 11 and 12? And poor old 1?) which was a plenty good letter with lots of laffs included.

But that picture! Honest, it actually took my breath away for a minute, you looking at me with those bright eyes of yours. It brought back a flood of memories all at once and made me wish I was on my way to Coronado already. I can't wait. At any rate, that little old picture has brightened up my whole life.

The sox are also breathtaking. I wouldn't believe you made them if you hadn't shown me some of your work in progress. Don't think they won't be appreciated or useful just because I'm not in a cold climate anymore. They remind me of you — they're just the

April 30, 1946, was a Tuesday. This letter was written either Tuesday, April 30, or Wednesday, May 1.

right size and are very soft and warm and comfortable. It amazes me that you'd go to so much trouble and work so on a present to me, whom you know so little about — you didn't even know whether I <u>wore</u> sox or not — but thank you, from the bottom of my feet — I mean heart.

I was also happy to hear that you have such a nice job. What's Dr. Latham like? He sounds like a wolf to me. I'm glad you didn't go to work with Thearle's Music Store, as I'm sure Thearle is nothing but a wolf.

I'm surprised you got the job with Dr. Latham — you said he wanted an assistant with no experience. Didn't you tell him about your first two husbands? That sounds like nice pay and hours, though — I have Wednesday and Saturday afternoons off, also. We should be together — we could have a lot of fun on Wednesday and Saturday afternoons, to say nothing of your $140 per mo.

Sounds like the Eliane-Clyde fiasco (sh-h-h!) has been taken off the front pages and is now back in the want ads somewhere. Whatever do you girls find not to talk about nowadays? You say you don't have any scandals? You say you need something juicy to liven up the old neighborhood? Tell ya what I'm goner dew — why don't you make out like you've got the love for me, and then I'll develop a wife and three children in Texas and tell Nancy and tell her not to tell you and then tell Eliane about it and tell her to tell you but to tell you not to tell Nancy that she told you what I told her to tell you — why, that'll keep their little minds occupied at the bridge table for months!

We may always fight about "Fibber McGee and Molly" but at least we agree on one kind of program — "Music for Dreaming" sounds pleasant. Maybe you'd even like F.M. & M if somebody like me (let's just say "me") was there to explain the jokes to you.

Sorry I couldn't clash you with you the cats vs. dogs topic, but here's an interesting point for debate: do you think people should beat their wives with a leather belt, or a bamboo cane? I'll have to admit I'm a little green on the subject, never having had any wives to beat; but despite the fact that you've had two husbands I think we can develop a lively argument on the subject.

I saw "A Song To Remember" the other night, with Merle Oberon and Paul Muni as F. Chopin. Huh?

Tonight I'm going across the island to see "Adventure" with C. Gable and G. Garson. Tomorrow night it's Margaret O'Brien and Boris Karloff in "Mad Love." Have you heard Joe Banana and his orchestra with appeal?

Well, adios for now, Painless Mathewson — watch those bicuspids.

Lots of love,
Jack

P.S. Thanks again for the sox, and the picture.

P.P.S. Don't you think I'm just a little bit dopey? It's very important, so answer quick like a fox.

HOLD THE PHONE! Just got a sensational letter from you dated Mar. 18 in Jacksonville, Fla. Must answer immediately, separate letter.

May 2

Beebe, darling,

I was just finishing up on the letter to you thanking you for the picture and sox when all of a sudden somebody drops <u>two</u> more letters from you in my lap. After blushing and thanking him, I find that one of them is from Jax (no kin to the beer of the same name), dated March 18, and is the most enjoyable piece of literature I ever read. I mean the one where you said you thought it was peachy of me to be in love with you and that you might even <u>possibly</u> might be the same. Obviously the girl got too much of that Florida sun, I says to myself after picking myself up off the floor. But it's wonderful to think about, and I feel like my head is up there at about 10,000 feet in the clouds. All I've got to say is, it couldn't have happened to a nicer fellow. No, that isn't <u>all</u> I've got to say, either — most of it'll have to wait till I see you again, as I couldn't begin to express it on paper.

You write the best letters I've ever read, no kidding. I've never saved anybody's letters before as I figure they just clutter up the joint and are trouble to carry around from place to place, but I've saved all of yours and read them over several times. Whenever I'm a little low and need a laugh, I can always pick up one of your letters and feel better. I think you'd probably have the same effect on me, personally.

How do you like the new job at the molar museum? Do you hold the patients' hands while the doc's drilling or do you just stroll around flashing your pretty white teeth in the customers' faces?

That idea of yours of swimming out to Pt. Loma to meet my ship is pretty good, but I plan to fly one of the squadron's planes back right to North Island when we finally get decommissioning orders. Wouldn't it be just as sensational for me to fly over the ferry and hook you in like they do mail-bags. And with that two-hour lunch period you have now, a mail-bag is what you're gonna resemble if you don't watch out. If you lose that shape of yours I shall be very discombooberated. But still in love with you, natch.

Now that you've got the job, you may not have time to knit me that sleeveless sweater, but I'm sending you the measurements anyhoo just in case you get around to it: (You asked for neck (Yes!), chest, waist, length, arm-hole, etc.)

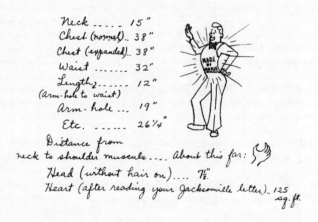

Neck ..... 15"
Chest (normal).. 38"
Chest (expanded).. 38"
Waist .... 32"
Length .... 12"
(arm-hole to waist)
Arm-hole ... 19"
Etc. ...... 26¼"
Distance from
neck to shoulder muscule .... About this far:
Head (without hair on).... 7⅛".
Heart (after reading your Jacksonville letter).. 125 sq. ft.

I hope I get some of those snapshots you were talking about. I'll try to get one to send you, although personally if you like the picture you have of me I really should let well enough alone and not try to force my luck too far. Speaking of pictures, somebody left the Grape-nuts out of the box with your picture. But it still looks good enough to eat, to me.

I have lots more to write you, honey, but I'll save it for the next letter which will follow shortly. I've gotta do <u>something</u> besides think of you!

All my love,
Jack

P.S. Am sealing this one with a lil bittie kiss instead of my usual big ol gooey one as that is the kind you asked for. But I'm not in favor of it.

You are cordially invited to attend

a party

given in honor of the Army and Navy Wives
of
Saipan - Marianas Islands
Special guest of honor

𝔐𝔯𝔰 - 𝔍𝔞𝔪𝔢𝔰 𝔊 - 𝔚𝔞𝔯𝔢

at the

Pacific Fleet Officers Mess
CAMP CALHOUN

on Saturday 4 May 1946
Cocktails and Dancing
from
2000 until 2330

Formal attire optional

SMOOCHIN ON THE
DANCE FLOOR STRICKLY
FORBIDEN

MARIE, MARIE, YOUR TEETH ARE SO WHITE,
COME ON, LET'S HOCK'EM AND STEP OUT TONITE.

KNIT ONE, PURL TWO;
BEEBE, YOO HOO!

HOPE THIS REACHES YOU IN TIME FOR YOU TO COME.
HOT TOMATO FROM CORONADO" FROM THE DOPEY ONE OF V H - 1."

Dear Hilarious,

Guess what I went out and played today! It's a peculiar game, somewhat like golf, and you play with a ball about the size of a golf ball, and you use clubs like in golf, and in fact I guess it was golf we were playing, but it didn't seem like it the way I played it. Yes, the Saipan Country Club is in the process of being constructed — they're hacking it out of the wilderness. That's also what I was doing today, hacking it out of the wilderness. They have nine holes, they tell me, but I didn't come close enough to see any of 'em. I shot about a 55 for the nine and then quit, figuring that gives me about an 85 for the eighteen as I was just getting warmed up when we quit.

Well, Cotton, our fourth monthly anniversary has just passed and here I am in the same condition as so vividly described to you in past issues of this publication. Still batty about you and wishing I were there or you were here or we both were anywhere in the same place. Even if you can't hold your popcorn till the

81

main feature and can't appreciate good hoomorous radio programs. I guess it must be your — personality. All I know is we go together like molasses and hot cakes.

Got a good letter from home, along with your two terrific bombshells yesterday. (Pardon me while I re-ink.) Remember the sister in New York who just finished dramatic school? It seems Broadway is not quite ripe for Sweeneys just yet, so instead of accepting the lead in "Tobacco Road" she let Kay Cornell (we call her Kay) have the part and landed a much better job as a receptionist (whatever that might be) for Richard Hudnut's Fifth Avenue Beauty Salon — I personally have never heard of the joint, but from the way Mother was steamed up over it, it's the bee's knees. She works from 5pm to 10pm, which sounds like nice hours, even to a Naval Officer. I can't imagine the little rascal in a job like that, but then we Sweeneys were always noted for our blind modesty.

And then another sister just unveiled the gruesome fact that she's been secretly married to her hometown beau since last <u>August!</u> Mother almost had a fit, naturally, which was what Peggy knew she would have and was scared to tell her because of it — not that Mother didn't like the boy, because she did, and so do I, but he's just a good old country boy who'll always be just that, and I think Mother thought Peggy could do better, or something. But after all, she's 22 (Peggy, not Mother) and should know what she wants. Come to think of it, you're 34, and do you? Anyhow, Mother reports that they seem to be as happy as if they had good sense, so I guess it'll be okay.

And then another sister (settle down, gal, I have five of 'em) has just gone back to Washington, D.C. to work for the C.A.A. (Don't ask me.) She has lived there quite a bit and seems to share your enthusiasm over Our Capital City. I also like it, I might add; but I won't, as there are too many women in this letter for me to get an edge in wordwise. Oh, just call me a little shaver, honey, I'm really sharp tonight!

At this point, I would like very much to be able to slip in a funny joke to relieve the boredom I'm no doubt causing you, but I can't think of one.

Horses should bet on people. It's lots of fun.

Dearest Ann,

I just won sixty bucks (10 dollars, at 6 to 1) on the Kentucky Derby and am so excited I had to tell somebody about it, and naturally it's you because I picked that good little old Texas horse Assault to win and knowing how you are always so enthusiastic about Texas and people and horses who come from there, I knew you'd like to know that our horse came in on top. Also I wanted to prove to you that that day at Santa Anita was just an off-day and that I know how to pick those horses after all, and I wanted to redeem myself, just as I will give <u>you</u> another chance at the bowling alley some day.

It seems funny to be listening to the big race on Sunday morning, but back there where you are it is Saturday afternoon and you're probably dolling yourself up this very minute to step out with some worthless wolf tonight — I mean this afternoon, where I am. It's very confoosin' but not very amoosin.'

85

KORNDORFER & CAPEZUTO

PLEASE OBSERVE FOUL LINE

THE SATURDAY EVENING POST

"Now try it!"

I can't understand why you didn't come to the big dance here last night, as I know I sent you an invitation two or three days ago. It was a gala event, with captains and commanders and generals and wives all over the place. It got to be pretty drunk up there, but I really couldn't blame most of the boys because if I were stuck on Saipan with the wives that some of them have I'd probably get plastered also. Honest, Cotton, if there had been one girl there with half your class and general all-around charm, she'd have been mobbed. There were about 300 officers there and less than 100 women. I got in a couple of steps in the arena, just to keep in practice for you, you know.

If we keep planning things we're going to do when

I get back, such as teach me the game of cribbage, bowling tournament, Pizza-hunting, etc., we'd better start a check-off list to make sure we don't skip anything. I've always wanted to learn cribbage, but I'll wait and let you show me so you can have the exquisite pleasure of beating me in something a couple of times before I catch on and start skunking you every time.

I heard a hot one at the dance last night — one fellow says to another fellow, "Boy, look at that evening dress — strapless and backless." And the other fellow says "Yeah, but most of them here tonight seem to be shapeless and hopeless." I confess it was me who said it and got a pretty good laugh, too, but I had heard it before somewhere.

All my love,
The dopey one of VH-1

Wednesday, May 8

Dear Gert,

I was very muchly surprised to get your short letter yesterday asking me to write your sister Marieosky. I appreciate your "interest" and think it is just too sweet of you to look after Marieosky's interests, but I want you to know you're not fooling me for one minuet. And it won't do you any good. You are obviously trying to beat Marieosky's time with me, but I see through that, as every year about this time there are literally dozens of designing females like you trying to scrape an acquaintance with me so I have had plenty of experience dealing with cases like yours. Not that I blame you, my dear comrade — it's not every mekushla (?) that gets a chance at a rich and handsome young man like I, but you are just too late, see. Your sister Marieosky has completely captivated me and when I fall, it makes quite a bang. And I am strictly a one-woman man, see, so naturally I am not the least bit interested in your advances. I shall follow Marieosky to the ends of the earth if necessary, and from what I have seen of some parts of California that may not be very far off.

Tough luck, Gertie, but that's life. Please understand that Marieosky is the only girl in my life and stop annoying me.

Sympathetically,
Jason

P.S. What's your phone number in case Marieosky is with another comrade when I arrive in Coronado?

Thursday, May 9

Hello, Love of my Life,

I have heard rumors recently that you weren't getting enough letters from me, so I searched back
through my files and sure enough there was a couple
of days in a row back there in April when I just
<u>thought</u> about writing you instead of doing it. That
was caused by the fact that your Florida letters (both
of 'em) were late in arriving and consequently I
didn't hear from you for a couple of weeks and so
didn't have much to talk about as it is hard for me to
talk long to anybody who doesn't talk back. Since
then you've been extra sweet, though, and I've had
plenty to write about although my letters may not
sound like it.

But what am I doing all this explaining for when
I've got something Big to tell you. The hot dope
around Saipan these days is that VH-1 is to be
decommissioned right away unless something goes
wrong, and that means we'll be winging our way

back to San Diego, possibly in a week or two. You know how the Navy is, you can't depend on 'em, but it really does look good.

I have been in a quandary as to whether to tell you in advance like this or just wait till I got to North Island, drop a nickel in the slot and dial H3-4792 and see what happened; but I decided to play safe and tell you so you will have plenty of time to brush off all the boy friends, save up a little gambling money, and clear the decks for action. You better have plenty of nickels handy. And straighten that lipstick.

This <u>could</u> be a false alarm, of course, nothing definite yet, but if I'm not haunting your doorstep within a couple of months at least, I'll beat my brains out with a banana stalk.

What do you hear from Glen? Did her coast-to-coast hookup come off as planned? The groom is probably calling it a cost-to-cost hookup. (I got a million 'em — a million of 'em!)

There are a surprising lot of families here on Saipan now, and they keep coming. I heard a lot of wives were coming in on a transport today and went down to the dock to draw one, but it seems there was already a man for every one of 'em — came out exactly even. It seems funny to see a bunch of white kids running around on Saipan. You don't realize how you miss seeing and being around good old American children till you don't see any for a few months. In China they're (the Chinese kids) all working all the time.

Got a report from headquarters that Katy, my youngest sister who is a junior in high school, is playing the lead in the school's contest play which is making theatrical history in the Texas high school play contests. Another Sweeney taking to the stage, although she's not serious about it like the one in New York. I guess dramatic talent runs in the family — even I once had my foot in a cast. (Joke.)

The demobilization is wiping us out. We now have only 20 men left in the squadron, which is one reason why it looks like we'll get orders to decommission soon. The shortage is so acute that I think they're going to make me a Patrol Plane Commander and I'll get to fly one of the planes back to San Diego myself.

Our skipper, Lt. Comdr. Gruber, lived with his family in Coronado for a month or so before coming out here and enjoys talking about that lovely community almost as much as I do. He keeps telling me about what a swell place to eat La Avenida is, and you never even took me there. I can't tell him exactly what it was about Coronado that made me think it was Paradise; I've seen much better golf courses and eaten in better places than the Colony and the Putt-Putt, and danced in better places than the world-famous Circus Room. All I remember is you, darling, and a better memory than that, I don't have.

Will let you know as soon as anything definite about decommissioning happens. Hope I get a big long letter from you tomorrow — I haven't heard how the new job turned out yet. Goodnight, honey-bunch.

Love,
Jack

Monday, May 14*

Darling,

Flash! VH-1 departs from sunny Saipan in the merry Marianas Thursday, May 23. Immediate destination, Kaneohe, Hawaii, by way of Wake and Johnston Islands. What happens to VH-1 after reaching Kaneohe, nobody knows; but there is a good chance of our being sent on to San Diego for decommissioning. There's also some talk of being sent to Norfolk, which wouldn't be so perfect but would help, as we'd have to go through San Diego. I'll try to call you from Kaneohe when we find out what's what.

I haven't heard from you in two weeks, except indirectly through your sister Gertie. You want to keep an eye on that Gertie, Beebe, because she's a female wolf if I ever saw one. And I'm so weak. But

*May 14, 1946, was a Tuesday. This letter was written either Monday, May 13, or Tuesday, May 14.

seriously, when I go two weeks without one of your sweet letters, my morale is crushed. You shouldn't do it to me.

Incidentally, just because I'm probably gone from Saipan when you get this, don't stop writing, puh-lease. I'll intercept them in Hawaii — we may be there for a week or so. And then again, we may only be there for a couple of days and then — on to Coronado! That's almost too good to think about, but I've certainly been doing a lot of thinking about it. I'm not counting on it <u>too</u> much, as I don't want to be disappointed if it falls through. But if <u>wanting</u> something badly enough counts for anything, then I'm practically there.

I had the best dream about you last night I've ever had.

All my love,
Jack

air mail

Wednesday, May 15

Beebe, darling,

No sooner did I ask for a letter than I got one. You seem to read my mind — how do you like it? No. 21 arrived today, and was one of your best. In a way, it was <u>the</u> best. The last one I got was #15, so some of them must've gone astray.

This one I got today was like something out of "Cass Timberlane" — all about the 62-year-old dentist and his playing around with his assistant. Personally I cannot understand why he wants to philander when he has a wife who plays a crack game of golf. If she topped her approaches or talked while he was lining up his putts, it might be excusable.

But seriously (I assume you were serious about your opinion of the whole affair and others like them — you're so rarely serious about anything, it's kinda hard for me to figure out just when you are) my views coincide exactly with yours on an old gink — or a young one — endangering his family's happiness by stepping out while the wife is home tending to her knitting. Some people do seem to have the idea that it's okay, I guess, but apparently I was brought up by the same kind of people you were, Beebe — people who believe that when two people are married, they're the same as one person, and everybody else is on the outside looking in. That's the kind of guy I am, anyway — I have lots of faults, I know (well, one or two maybe) but I'm certain that disloyalty to my wife or family will never be one of them. When I get married, that is.

When you said your father was the best man you have known, with the exception of me, I'm sure you must've been indulging in a bit of joshing, Blondie, as you can't know me well enough to say that — but it was the finest compliment I've ever received and I hope I can prove you're right.

I'm like you, Beebe — when I suddenly see something like the Affair of the Dentist and his Assistant, it disgusts me. I've often wondered, from seeing so many examples of infidelity in recent years, whether it's a product of war hysteria or whether it's been going on all the time and I've only become aware of it since growing up. I've come to the conclusion it's been like that with husbands and wives since Adam & Eve, but I'm still not in favor of it, and judging from your letter you're not either. And I can't tell you how glad I am. In fact, every letter I get from you convinces me more that you're the kind of girl I hope you are.

I wish we could talk with each other about things like this instead of having to write it — by the time I answer your letter it's a month later and the subject's cold. If only they send us to San Diego for decommissioning (you're so right, it _is_ a long word). As I wrote you yesterday, we won't know until we get to Kaneohe May 23, at which time (or as soon as we find out) I'll call you up and let you know. It'll certainly be great to hear your voice again.

I hope the letter with the snapshots you're sending me doesn't get off on the plane to Shanghai, as letters #16, 17, 18, 19, and 20 must have done. Also #1 and #11.

No I haven't read "The Egg and I" so will restrain myself from doing so till you present me with an autographed copy. Make mine over, easy.

Soup without noodles may be tasteless, honey, but noodles without soup is ridiculous. And don't you forget it.

I love you too much,
Jack

Darling,

Here I am again. Honest, I've never been like this before in my life — if I'm not mistaken, this is the third day in a row I've written you, and I always thought guys who wrote every day were nuts. Writing you is the next best thing to (1) being with you or (2) reading a letter from you, and since I can't do either (1) or (2) right now, I'll write a little nonsense.

I saw a movie tonight that took me right back to January 1, 1946 — it was just a fair movie, "Up Goes Maisie" with Ann Sothern of course, but the best part of it was that Ann Sothern and George Murphy were demonstrating their new sensational helicopter in the Rose Bowl, and some of the pictures were taken right from where we were sitting on that momentous occasion. Which is to say, from way down there in the end zone, but after all, on such short notice how could I get better seats and anyway I didn't know I was going to have a gorgeous blonde with me (on whom I wanted to make a big impression) at the time I bought the tickets.

Perry Como is now singing "Don't Blame Me" which takes me back to Camp Kidd December 31, 1945. Everything seems to take me back to something which reminds me of you and the wonderful two weeks we had together. I wish a big old PBM airplane would take me back. And it might do just that, if my horoscope is clicking when we get to Kaneohe about a week from now. I never wanted anything so intensely in my life.

Tomorrow night the skipper is taking me out on a night flight to see if I know what the score is on night-flying, and if I pass O.K., he may qualify me as P.P.C., which, as I told you, is what I want most in this world next to you.

Then Thursday or Friday (23rd or 24th) we leave for Kaneohe to find out whether we go to San Diego for decommissioning or not. It may be a couple of days before we find out, so it may be Sunday or Monday before I call you up.

I have taken up tennis with a bang the past week, the bang being the sound made by the ball hitting the wood instead of the strings on my racket usually, but I'm enjoying getting back to the sport in which I once thought I would be the World's Interscholastic Champion of. But they wouldn't let me on the high school team so I never got a chance to show my skill throughout the country.

In that movie tonight Ann Sothern was trying to fly this helicopter out to the Rose Bowl and was having a heck of a time getting out there. She should've seen me trying to pilot that brakeless Ford out there on New Year's Day at high noon, and she wouldn't have been so proud of what she did.

I see the communists are fighting just 85 miles from Tsingtao, China now — glad we got out of there. I was flying around here the other day and picked out a beautiful little island where I think I'll run off to and settle down when the next atomic bombs start falling. I'd like to have you along, sweetheart, but you'll have to bring your own radio.

All my love,
Jack

P.S. I wish I had an Old-Fashioned — because if I did, you'd be sitting on the other side of it.

Saipan, Satiddy, May 18

Dearest Beebe,

If you haven't gotten that sensational trans-
oceanic phone call from me yet, just keep on standing
by to stand by — I'll get through any day now.
Determination, perseverance, and PBM's will get me
there yet. I won't be leaving Saipan till next Saturday
at least, which means I won't get to Kaneohe till
Monday or Tuesday (27th or 28th), so possibly it'll
be the 29th or 30th before I get the call through.

I got No. 22 from you today, with three snapshots.
(Missing: #1, 19, and 20.) It was sweet of you to send
'em to me, honey — I love that sunny smile of yours.
Pardon my French, but my dear, aren't you putting
on a bit of avoirdupois since I was there? My roommate has been arguing with me (still is, right now)
that you are just being witty and sending me somebody else's picture — he says he can't believe that
the snapshots are the same girl that Lou Goodale
Bigelow photographed and whose beautiful face

103

smiles at me from atop my locker. I <u>knew</u> that two-hour lunch period was a mistake.

Speaking of French, one of these days I'm gonna get somebody who speaks the stuff and get him to tell me what all those French words mean that you stick in your letters to me. I heard some in the movie the other night that I didn't savvy but the way the gal said it, it sounds safe to say it to you — parlez moy dah moor, Madam Zelle.

After seeing those snapshots, I've started wondering if <u>I</u>'ve changed any since we were together. Of course a person can't see himself change any, but maybe one changes while one isn't looking, doesn't one? I'll tell you one change, though — since your father and I can't make you quit smoking so much, I decided to take it up in a violent way — nothing but big ole nasty cigars. Just watch my smoke! I'll smoke you out yet.

I almost turned a flip reading your No. 17 letter, darling — yes, you can file your carbon copies of that one under the caption, "This Is My Best." It was the most wonderful letter I've ever read, along with No. 7 from Jacksonville, and said just what I wanted to hear.

Everybody in the squadron is on pins and needles wondering what orders we'll get at Kaneohe. Will we go on to San Diego, will we get decommissioned in Kaneohe instead and sent back out to another squadron, or will we just be sent back out anyhow? Just sit back, folks, and tune in again next week, same time, same station and hear the next thrilling episode. Will John and Marie be re-united for more of their hilarious adventures up and down the West Coast of the U.S.A.? We don't know, folks, but meanwhile, why not buy Poopsy Popsy Pop Corn — the Pop Corn that automatically pops itself when the main feature comes on — you can't eat it till then, no matter what!

I got by the night-flying episode I was telling you about with only a few minor crashes and so things look rosy along that line. I mean, I'll soon be a P.P.C., which ranks somewhere between an admiral and a dentist.

I saw a swell movie the other night — "Sailor Takes a Wife" with Robert Walker and June Allyson. It's a riot — you must see it when it gets around to Coronado.

I miss you more than I can say, honey — I'm really eager to get back and take up where we left off — or did we?

Te quiero y buenas noches, senorita Maria
(so there, too),
Don Juan

P.S. After reading this over, thought I'd better add this — if what I said about your making like Sophie Tucker was too fresh, I'm sorry. But it's not as if I were only casually interested in you. You mean everything to me. And it's only natural that I want you not to change while I'm gone — I want you to be the same Beebe I took to the Rose Bowl and Camp K. and home that last night — same wit, same kisses and same dimensions — because they were perfect for me!

Hello, honya,

Onesy, twosy, I love yousy. I got No. 23 yesterday. You're really right in the groove lately with the letters. It's a swell feeling to see that stack of mail come into the squadron office two or three times a week and know there's going to be one or maybe two of those blue envelopes in there for me with all that sweet stuff inside. I don't know what I'd do or what I'd be thinking about all the time if I didn't have that to look forward to.

Still getting ready to get ready to fly east Saturday. And here's hoping we don't stop at Kaneohe.

You asked me if I played bridge — don't you read my letters? Didn't I write you how I was probably the leading bridge expert in the country? And there ain't many in the city that can beat me, either. If I get the cards.

I also told you that when I was with you that I

107

belonged to the same church you did — you must learn to pay attention when the Sahib is speaking, dear.

I may as well deal you all the pertinent facts about me so we can have more stuff to argue about now that they have jolted "This is My Best" down into the afternoon soap opera category. I'm an Episcopalian, Democrat, Texan, Irish, bat right-handed, throw right-handed, detest cauliflower and sweet potatoes, and took an oath when I was five years old to devote my life to making blondes happy.

Gotta cut this short, darling, to get it in the morning mail.

All my love,
Jackson

P.S. "A.B.S."?
A Big Smooch, maybe?
Always Beat Sweeney?
Always, Beebe's Second?
Adieu, Bon Sherry (French)

Darling,

This letter-writing is getting to be a habit, or something. It's just like you say — when I'm writing you, it's almost as if I were talking to you, I feel so close to you. But it still would be so much nicer to be with you in person, to be able to just touch you, to hold you in my arms like that last night before I left. I guess I've thought of those short hours a thousand times in the past four months.

Saturday will come some day, I suppose, but it's certainly taking its good old time getting here. That's the day I leave sunny Saipan for Kaneohe and <u>possibly</u> points east.

I've tried to imagine what it'll be like if I <u>do</u> get to go on to San Diego and run up to your front door and yell to see if Beebe's there. We have so many things to do and talk about, how will we start? I thought maybe it'd be a good idea to start where we said goodbye and do everything we did before only backwards, but if we did that we'd wind up at a squadron party at the club practically strangers, and that's not what I have in mind at all. Besides, the Coronado golf course might not like for us to start in at the ninth hole and end up at putting on the first tee.

Glad to hear Danny boy and his gal have reached an agreement. So you bane Norwegian, ya? Curses, I thinking you bane Roosian and I bane gone taking you back to Wladiwostok to halp find true fodder. (Sorry, I washed my fountain pen today and can't do a thing with it!) Skohl! (Sp?)

Also glad your job is keeping you busy, but watch your step in that dark room with those x-rays. I got a hunch that old wolf of a dentist ain't paying you 140 bucks just to lend atmosphere to the office. Take good care of yourself, sweetheart — I love you. Truly.

Love,
Jack

P.S. Glad you like my "wonderful smile" — here's a picture of it just for you:

 (¼ life size)

Friday, May 31

Beebe darlint,

I am now writing you from the Women Officers Quarters at Kaneohe Naval Air Station. Now, put down that rolling pin, love, I can explain everything. It seems they are short of space over in the main Bachelors' Officers Quarters and long of it here since so many Waves have gone home from fighting the war, so they have moved all the females over into one wing of the building and we live in this wing, temporarily. I mean until we get into the main B.O.Q.

We got here Tuesday but still are wondering what they're going to do with us. Some say we'll be decommissioned in Norfolk; some (including me) say San Diego; and some say we'll have "permanent" duty here at Kaneohe. We may find out something in a day or two in which case you'll already know by the time you get this letter as I intend to call you up and tell you personally. The personal touch, y'know.

The married boys are all hoping we get the permanent duty here so they can send for their families and settle down. I can see their point — this would be a wonderful place to live for the next year or two while these United States are squaring themselves away with labor and housing shortages and food (but need I go on?).

It seems like months since I've written you, honeybunch. It's really been only a week, and it's been a busy one. I've flown about 4,000 miles since I wrote you last, so I'm now only 2,100 miles away from you. Closer than if I were on the east coast. I got Letter No. 25 the day I left Saipan but have been lonesome for one ever since. Your letters affect my morale exactly like you say mine do yours. What is this thing called love? (From the picture of the same name.) I still haven't seen #19 or #24. Or of course, #1 which I'm beginning to give up hope on.

Believe me, Hawaii has never looked so beautiful to me as it does right now. It's funny, but it seems like the way Hawaii impresses me depends on which way I'm going — when I'm on my way west, it's not so hot because I've just left the states and Hawaii represents the tropics and boredom I'm heading for. But when I'm on the way back, such as now, it represents civilization — good food, better living conditions, etc. However, no matter which way it is, I don't think anyone would doubt that the view I have out my window right now is hard to beat. Far be me from it to attempt a description but just let me say that the W.O.Q. is up on this hill and I can look out over the whole base (which is even larger than North Island's) and on the other side is the bay, which has water like you see on picture postcards, and in the background we have some big rugged mountains, and taking it all around, it is a very nice arrangement indeed.

And on the inside of the room, there is naturally a gorgeous picture of Beatrice Bernadette Mathewson atop my dresser, which makes the scenery <u>inside</u> the room even more interesting than the stuff on the outside I was talking about.

I'm enjoying getting back to a lot of the little things in life I've been missing. Fresh milk, fresh vegetables, salads, soft bed, and many others. (Oh yes — the smell of foo-foo on the women-folks — how's your Chanel No. 5 holding out?) (Save a drop or two to use on me, tho I'm sure you won't need it.)

Dearest Beebe,

Greetings, my scandalous Scandinavian. I just got back from my first social activity since leaving San Diego (unless you count Shanghai, and let's not) and I missed you so much over there at that dance that I thought I'd like to write you before turning in. If it's a little more crazy than usual, please bear in mind that I've had about eight or nine Toms Collin tonight and am apt to do or say something radical, under such circumstances.

The social activity mentioned in paragraph (1) was a dance at the Officers Club, and let me state at this point that the Kaneohe Officers Club is one of the most beautiful I've ever seen. They had a swell band there, the floor was perfect, the breeze was blowing off the blue Pacific, the stars were twinkling overhead — but alas, the whole thing was a dreary affair for me because Beebe wasn't with me. I did dance a couple of dances with somebody named

115

Gladys, but I can't fool anybody when I've got the love so I gave it up and came back to my room, so I could look at your picture and write you a letter. (I know — so far I haven't said anything, but give me time!)

Well, they told us yesterday what they had in store for VH-1. I shall try to call you Monday, but in case I don't get through, here's the gruesome facts: VH-1 will remain in Kaneohe until Sept. 1, at least — after that, nobody knows; but my guess — and hope — is that we get sent back to San Diego for decom. then. Will you keep writing me, pretty please?

I haven't had a letter from you since I left Saipan but it may not be your fault — the mail hasn't been straightened out and some of it's probably still going to Saipan. But I wish I had a letter from you.

I'm certainly looking forward to that phone call Monday — one of the boys called his wife when we first arrived and said the connection was awfully bad — like short-wave radio — but if I can hear you at all, it'll be worth it.

By the way, that same boy who called his wife has bought a house in Coronado and we were talking the other day and naturally I was talking about you and it turned out that he had talked to your father once about taxes on his house.

I hope you feel better about your job by now or quit the darn thing. I can't stand thinking about your being unhappy about anything, and the last letter I got from you sounded as if you weren't at all satisfied with the way your job was going. Why don't you save up a couple of months' pay and quit and take a vacation in — let us say — Hawaii? I miss you, darling.

All my love,
Jack

Monday, June 3

Dearest Beebe,

Just got back from that confoosin' but very amoosin' trans-oceanic coast-to-coast Sweeney-to-Mathewson telephone conversation. I don't know what we said, but I got a big bang out of whatever it was. My shorthand expert was along and took it all down for the newspapers and here's what came off, according to him:

OPERATOR: Go ahead.

JACK: Hello — Beebe?

BEEBE: What?

JACK: Hello — is that you, Beebe?

BEEBE: Okay.

OPERATOR: You have one minute left.

JACK: What happened to the first four minutes?

BEEBE: What?

JACK: I think you're the most wonderful girl I've

118

ever known, and I adore you, honey.

BEEBE: Huh?

JACK: I said how much weight have you gained?

OPERATOR: What?

BEEBE: Why you — gribble smock diffuser gamble sweater.

JACK: What did you say about the sweater?

BEEBE: Huh?

JACK: Are you mad at me?

BEEBE: Naturally.

OPERATOR: Yer five minutes is up. Tell 'er goodbye.

JACK: Huh?

OPERATOR: Goodbye, Beebe. (Hangs up.) That'll be $734.26, Mr. Sweeney.

(End of conversation)

Well, that's the last time I'll spend $734.26 on a trans-oceanic phone call, even to you. Unless something big comes up. I could hear you fairly well, but you weren't receiving me. I'd say something clever as

119

the dickens, and you'd ask for a repeat, and by the third time I'd said it, I'd decided it wasn't so funny after all, and off I'd go on another tack. But all in all, I enjoyed it a lot and it was swell hearing you again. That was the shortest five minutes I ever saw. Next time I'll ask for ten.

All my love,
Jack

Darling,

I wish I knew whether you're kidding about quitting work on that sweater or not. You see, I've been knitting myself a beret to wear with it, and would like to know whether to continue or not. Besides, I don't think you ought to be mad at me just for asking if you'd gained some poundage since I left because all I wanted was to be sure I could still put my arms all the way around you and besides you did look different with your hair on top of your head, you must admit, and anyway I'd like it less if you'd <u>lost</u> any weight, but anyway what has weight to do with true love, I always say. Isn't that what you always say? Oh.

I was awfully disappointed when I heard we'd be here till Sept. 1, but that's only three more months and then we're pretty sure of going on to the states. I hope you won't give up on me and start slowing up on the letters, as I look forward to them more than anything.

I went over to Honolulu the other day. The most interesting part of the trip was the bus ride over the Pali, which is what they call the mountain pass you go through to cross the mountains between Kaneohe and the city. That bus ride beats any roller coaster I ever rode, for thrills. I think the time spent on that bus should be counted as flight time.

Sorry, Blondie, but my old eyes just won't stay open. More tomorrow. Goodnight, sweetheart.

Thursday

I've got the blues again today, so maybe it's better I should just sign this sad letter and send it where I wish I was. I've got a right to sing the blues — (1) I'm stuck here for three months, (2) no letter from you for twelve days, (3) am snowed under with paper work — our squadron has demobilized 52 men this month, including our yeoman, and I'm Personnel Officer, and a Personnel Officer without a yeoman is worse than a dentist without a dental assistant. You should see me at the office hour after hour plugging away at the typewriter, trying to get our reports off. But to get back to the blues, (4) my dreamboat is mad at me for practically no reason whatever. But if it will make you stop seething, I will apologize and admit that I'm a cad and a bounder, and if I ever remark on the fact that you may have added an ounce or two here and there again I hope I may be struck down on the spot, and probably will be if you are around at the time.

I told you I should've signed off before. Ta-ta for now.

Apologetically,
Jack

P.S. I get KNX Los Angeles on my radio.

My darling,

Well, Hallelujah! FOUR letters — ranging from April 28 to May 27 — came home today and the world looks much different. One was sealed with a kiss, one was sealed with a Big kiss, one was sealed with a peck (?), and one was just sealed, which means I got spit on. <u>That</u> I don't deserve, however free I may have been with loose remarks around about snapshots looking a teensy-weensy bit overweight. May my tongue be cut out and roasted over a slow fire if I ever make such a horrible mistake again.

The aforesaid letters had much variety — (1) some were enthusiastic, (2) some grumbled a little about not receiving any letters in the past 24 hours, (3) some romanced, and (4) some sizzled with indignation.

Taking up the various categories in order, (1) were read with regret that your optimism about my return was let down, (2) were read with sympathy and understanding, (3) were read with fast-beating heart and a glow of love (there — I've said it again mad, impetuous fool that I am!), and (4) were read with laughter, shame, relief, and a Milky Way candy bar. (If you can't make sense out of this, it serves you right, Blondie.)

Our situation changes from hour to hour here. I hesitated to write you because I'd like to tell you something definite, but it may be a week before that will be possible, so I'll keep firing letters at you as the Navy changes its mind.

The first tumultuous development in the past 24 hours is the crushing announcement that the squadron, instead of being here until Sept. 1 as I told you, will be decommissioned immediately — in Kaneohe! Wouldn't that curl your teeth? I have very little hope now of getting back to you any time soon, but there is one (or two) ray(s) of hope. One is that I may be able to talk my way back to shore duty in the United States, in which case everything would be rosy. But the chance isn't too good — they'll probably want to send me to another squadron out here somewhere (g-r-r-r!). The other possible ray of hope is that they may keep us around here to ferry planes to the coast, in which at least I'd get to see you.

But as I say, things change from hour to hour. My next letter to you will probably say something entirely different. One thing is certain — we're decommissioningingioningphooey the squadron <u>here</u> and as of about June 15, there will be no more VH-1. So don't write to VH-1 address any more — write to "Fleet Air Wing 2, NAS #28, c/o FPO," etc. But write, honey — it's awful to be without your letters even for a few days.

Getting back to your sizzling letter, I hope it won't <u>have</u> to be a thrilling kiss to make everything copasetti between us again, as it is a very long distance between us for that sort of thing, and even if I were there with you, I've probably forgotten how to do such things. It's been a long, long time since January 9. (Or rather, since the morning of the 10th.)

Just a little practice would probably be all I'd need, however. (Or maybe a lot, now that I think of it.)

It was perzactly 5 months ago today that we went to the movies in the afternoon ("Hold that Blonde"), <u>I</u> bowled ("Hold that Blonde," shouted the pin boy),

126

we returned late for dinner (and was that rabbit good!), and I handed you a terrific beating at gin rummy mostly through superior skill and because there was a nickel riding on the outcome. You see, I go to a church which believes card-playing is wicked, when you lose.

That was a wonderful day. I've known several girls who were fun to be with in the evening, but you are the first I've ever enjoyed being with all through the day. I kind of like you at night, too, you know.

I love, you,
Jack

Saturday, June 8
(RED LETTER DAY)

Dearest Beebe,

Stand by for latest flash: FLASH! SWEENEY RETURNING TO GIRL HE LEFT BEHIND!! And I'm not kidding, either. I told you things changed fast around here and I got the word practically from the Admiral's mouth(piece) this morning that I would get orders to report to San Diego for reassignment when VH-1 decommissions, which means about two weeks (or probably three, since I'll probably go by ship) from now (<u>about</u> July 1) I'll be pointing out Mars and Saturn to you again, with maybe a bit of courting thrown in on the side, hm?

All morning I've been going around in a daze humming "I'm Gonna See My Baby." I can hardly believe it yet.

My biggest worry now, aside from The One about whether you'll still love me when we're together again (they're now playing the song you told me about, "They Say It's Wonderful") (first time I've heard it) (it's nice) well, as I was saying, my big worry is — I haven't a <u>thing</u> to wear, my deah. I shall have to lay in a new wardrobe when I reach Sandy Ago. Can you possibly love a tramp who can't break $100? (I can play poker like a fiend, tho — won 40 skins last evening.) (Also card tricks done cheap.)

I am gonna be busy as a one-armed paperhanger next week writing orders for all the officers and men in the squadron and helping decommission, so I may not have much time for writing but will try to shoot a fast one to you whenever I can, keeping you posted on when you can start your swim out to Point Loma to meet my ship. (Ref. BBM letter dates Apr. 15, 1946.) This is Saturday but I gotta work all afternoon and maybe Sunday. Adios, my love.

With much adoration,
Jason

Darling,

Letter #31 came in (sealed with a Torrid kiss?) yesterday in record time and made me feel swell not only from what it said but also because I now have Letters #27, 29, and 30 to look forward to, as well as #1, bless its little heart.

Mr. Anthony, sir, may I say one or two words in defense. This young lady, whose initials are B.B., has misrepresented the facts maliciously and knowingly. She would have your honor believe that she has been doing nothing but writing a steady stream of letters to the accused ever since this correspondence started and that he sits back on his big PBM and casually tosses off a little note every month or so while she pines away hoping he will write more often. Ha! Mr. A., as man to man I am here to say that I have never done so much concentrated writing to a woman in my life as I have at that — that — assistant to a gum-cultivator. (Order in the court — order in the court!) Well, it's the honest tooth, yer honor. If only I had numbered my letters as she has, the facts would speak for themselves. Defense rests.

Well, ladies and gentlemen, this case seems to be very unique, as well as different. Here we have a beautiful, charming tomato and a clever, dopey drip who are obviously in love with each other, hurling accusations at one another when really they should be whispering sweet nyathings in each other's ears. Since this is muy difficult in their present locations, court hereby decrees that said correspondence, which is causing all the trouble, be brought to a halt, as of next month. In other words, get together! Next case.

Thank you, Mr. Anthony. That should solve <u>that</u> problem, although it may cause a few other interesting ones.

Am now reading "Madame Bovary" whenever I get a chance — will give you a complete review with expert opinion when I finish. Goodnight, angel.

Love, Jack

Tuesday

Honey chile,

Your letters are getting sweeter and sweeter, and my sweater is getting longer and longer, and my dreams are getting better all the time. Situation still the same, although I still haven't got my meathooks on those precious orders yet. It still looks like I'll be leaving here on a ship in about a week or ten days and pulling you out of the water near Pt. Loma around the last of the month or 1st of July.

Got Nos. 27 and 30 yestiddy — no #29 yet. No. 27 was sealed with a Beebe kiss, which almost knocked me out, unprepared as I was for it. You got to be in training for those things.

Now, students, back to "The Case of the Delinquent Dental Assistant," or —

"Dr. Latham's Love Life," or — "A Scientific Study of the Sex Life of a Dental Assistant," or — "She Was Only a Dental Assistant, But She Knew Which Side Her Filling Was Amalgamed On." I thought we'd already filed that case away in the archives, but it seems our lovely Lorelei has uncovered new evidence for the sahib. Well, it's clear that before I can delve into this case I'll have to be furnished a picture of the delinquent d.a., her phone number, and a daily list of Dr. L's dental appointments.

All kidding aside, though (honest, darling, <u>you're</u> the only dental assistant in my life) (in fact, you're the only girl in my life) (in fact, you're my life). But this could go on indefinitely — what I mean is, you can probably see the affair from a woman's viewpoint better than I and thus have reason to sympathize with her, but personally I can't see much to admire in that dental assistant. I know if I were her daughter, for instance, I'd be ashamed to be going through UCLA by such means. <u>I'd</u> even be ashamed of going through USC, by any means, but then I saw their football team and so I'm prejudiced. But that girl can't be very proud of her mother, and family pride is the finest thing in the world, to my way of thinking. As for Doc Latham, it's inexcusable for an old gink like that to turn to a younger woman just because the girl he married made the mistake of growing old with him. And that's me rulin' — next case!

Editor's note — the opinions expressed in this article are purely the views of the author and do not in any way reflect those of the U.S. Navy.

If I were a swallow, I'd go back to Capistrano, turn right on Highway 101, get on the Coronado ferry, and build my nest right outside your window. Ain't that sweet?

Wednesday morning —

Good morning, darling — I'm sorry I didn't get to finish this last night, but I wanted to write some more on it and didn't have time. I hate to mail you a short letter as yours are usually so long and sweet.

The day when we'll be together again is getting so close I'm getting a little scared. Just two, maybe three weeks. We've got a thousand things to do and talk about.

Meanwhile, I'm working my pore ol haid to the bone putting this squadron out of commission. And when the job is finished, I'm going to Californy and decommission a certain blonde I know.

All my love to you, sweetheart,
Jack

Dearest 🐾🐾

I've got to confess I'm not doing my bit in this correspondence of ours, Cotton — you're hard to keep up with when you finally get started. Yesterday, for instance, I got two more letters from you, including the one telling me about how old Doc Latham gave you the pink slip.

Darling, I wish I'd been there. If nothing else, I could have offered you fifty or sixty reasons why you didn't want the job anyway. From the first I could see that Dr. L. had no character whatsoever, even if he is a friend of the family.

I have several ideas about why you were really fired, none of which are very flattering to Dr. Latham or his assistants. I also have an idea that you're not still upset over it as you were when you wrote me and in fact you're probably not even bitter about it.

Personally I am thinking about getting a dental appointment with the old chromo when I get to Coronado and when he bends over and peers into my mouth I shall go "Ach-tooey" right in his face. But let's forget it — we'll have much more important things to do when I get to Coronado.

The enclosed photograph is not a recent one — as a matter of fact, it was taken on the U.S.S. Curtiss in Okinawa on January 27, just two and a half weeks after we parted. I am the one on the left. Since then I have grown much richer and handsomer. As you see by the triumphant sneer on my face, and by the bewildered, puzzled look on my opponent's face (Bob Gillock), Sweeney has once more conquered and has complete control of the situation on the Acey-Deucy Board.

I hear Jane Russell has been selected for the lead in the movie version of your favorite radio program, "This is my Bust."

My orders came in today. They can't keep me away from you now, honeybunch — I'll see you in about three weeks, at the latest — <u>possibly</u> even next week, if I can fly. Stand by for B-B Day!

Anticipatingly,
Jack

Tuesday, June 18

My darling,

VH-1 is no more, and now all I have to do is wait for transportation back to the Newnited Snapes, which seems to be in such a befuddled condition with nobody having any meat to eat or houses to live in that I am ashamed of myself for having stayed away so long and allowed everything to go to the dogs. (No, I am not talking about you, honey bunny boo.)

The transportation situation is like everything else in the Navy — it changes hourly. Yesterday I was all packed and ready to board a ship which would have had me in your arms in a week's time — today the news is that we're too far down the waiting list to get that ship and the next one is a gorgeous transport which, however, doesn't leave until the 26th. And all these ships go into San Francisco, which is a pretty far swim even for one of your abilities, so I guess your projected swim out to Point Loma will have to be called off and all money collected in the advance ticket sale cheerfully refunded. Now what will happen is that as soon as we hit Frisco I shall board the next available train or plane and you will have to do nothing more sensational than be waitin' for the train to come in. Or plane.

Which brings up a little point I should like to discuss briefly with you, Beebe. You know, we only really knew each other for two weeks, although I'm sure we came to know each other better in those two weeks than any other couple could. It's been five months since those two weeks came off, and all you've had in that time were my picture (and pictures like that are nearly always flattering) and my letters, in which I also try to flatter myself. In these five months you're bound to have gradually exaggerated my good features in your mind and more or less forgotten the bad ones (honest, I do have one or two bad ones — but there I go again). Probably you realize all this, honey, as I've suspected from the first you are not such a girl as would overlook such common-sense things. The reason I'm being so serious about it is that just in case you <u>do</u> feel some sense of disappointment when the highly-advertised Sweeney steps off his train (or plane), just be sure to remember that the main thing is what we're like <u>inside</u> and what we feel about things, etc. I'm sure you know what I'm trying to get across even if I'm not expressing it too clearly.

Yesterday I played golf for the second time since we got here. A <u>little</u> improvement was noted by the spectators, although it was frequently heard in the gallery that "Sweeney's still off his game." Shot a 50 on the first nine and 41 on the back side, for a 91. That's ten strokes off my last score, so anyone with a mathematical mind can see that if I play twice more I will be shooting a 71. Incidentally, one reason for the difference between the 50 and 41 was that my good friend Rasmussen (a Dane) came out to the course late and met me between the 9th and 10th holes with a letter (#35) for me from you. Despite my curiosity over what "SWMS" meant, my frame of mind was such that I really burned up the course from there on in. (Sealed With Many Smooches?)

This Rasmussen is my best friend in the Navy and has been for seven years. We roomed together at the Academy from the day we entered to the day we graduated. He is from the great metropolis of Seadrift, Texas. He just came in from the States and is on his way out just as I was in January. He was very blue about it as he has been engaged to a girl in Australia ever since his ship was there in 1943, and she has never been able to get transportation to the U.S.A. until this month — and here he is on his way to some rock in the Pacific! However, love will be triumphant, as he has talked the big boys into putting him into a squadron based here at Kaneohe. So now it's all fixed for her to fly here right away and the wedding bells will finally ring after all these years. "Life Can Be Beautiful!"

Wednesday, June 19

I'm getting lazy, darling — couldn't even get up the energy to go over and mail this letter last night. This is pretty soft, just lying around reading and listening to the radio and playing golf now and then. But I deserve it; the past three weeks have made me work harder than I ever did before.

Today is my fourth anniversary of graduation from the Naval Academy. It is also the day Billy

Conn and Joe Louis fight for the heavyweight champeenship of the world. You remember I told you about winning sixty dollars on the Kentucky Derby? Well, having a guilty conscience over having won all that moola from a good friend of mine by betting on a sure thing (the Texas horse), I decided to let him win it back from me by letting him bet me that amount on Joe Louis, me putting my money on Billy Conn who naturally does not have a chance. But at least it will make my friend feel good and I will be no worse off than I was before the horse race. Which is to say, very well off indeed, because no matter what setbacks I receive, I can just laugh it off and say, well there's always Beebe. It's nice to have something like that to say, because as long as I can say that I'll never feel _very_ badly about anything, see?

It won't be long now, sweetheart. I'll be seeing you.

All my love to you,
Jack

Dearest 🐝 🐝

How is my nutty Norsewoman? Probably getting tired of waiting for my arrival with baited breath. Hereafter permission is granted for you to wait with only half-baited breath.

Well, Billy Conn got wiped out by Joe Louis and the money I won on the Kentucky Derby goes back to its original owner, but there's always Beebe. So I'm cryin' on the outside and laughin' on the inside. Which reminds me — have you heard "I Don't Know Enough About You?" The title has nothing to do with us, but I heard P. Como sing it yesterday and thought it was really pretty.

I just got back from the movie. On a base like this, where there isn't much doing at night, everybody gets into the habit of going to the movie every night almost, no matter what it happens to be. Tonight it was a pretty good one — "Wells Fargo" — about ten years old and I think I saw it when I was in high school, but I'd rather see a good old one than a sorry new one, even if I've seen it before.

I played bridge a couple of nights ago (and won, of

143

course) with Ras, my old roommate, and enjoyed it a lot. He's some character, and I hope you meet him some day.

I'm still thinking of you all the time, honey. I know I've never looked forward to anything like I am to our coming celebration. This is the first day of summer, and it's likely to turn out to be a very memorable summer. I don't see how we can miss!

All my love,

P.S. I'm sorry I waited so long to mail this — will write again quick like fox.

Whatcha know, Jo?

or

What's knittin', kitten?

Don't look now, but that postman's doing things to us again — I got your letter #36 only today. That letter had almost as hard a time getting here as I'm having getting there.

So you lost three bucks on the fight. I don't remember telling you to put any money down on that prognostication of mine last January, so it's your own fault, and I refuse to be held responsible for your gambling debts. Personally, I'm sticking to horses from here on. At least they give you a run for your money. I'll never bet on Billy Conn again, unless they put him in a foot race with Joe Louis chasing him.

I'll probably hear from you and Mr. Anthony again in regard to my failure to write very often lately and I'll deserve every bit of it. You're so sweet with your letters that I should spend a lot more time trying to write you a good letter, but I guess I've just gotten lazy in letter-writing as well as everything else since the squadron was decommissioned and I knocked off work. I hope the flowers I sent about a week ago compensated a little for the scarcity of letters. (You <u>did</u> get some flowers, I hope — if not let me know quick so I can get my thirty cents back.)

From now on in my letters I'll put a quick summary of the transportation situation at the top of my letters so my reader can tell at a glance what the current dope is without having to shuffle through the many pages of the manuscript to find out. Then, if the reader feels like reading the rest of the literature she can peruse it casually over her morning calories and coffee.

I hope I make it back in time for that July full moon about the 15th. They do say such things are a definite advantage when a feller comes a-courtin'.

I appreciated the congratulations over my making P.P.C. [Patrol Plane Commander] and your expression of relief at finding that I wasn't so (quote) "moronic and screwy" (unquote) as believed before, but the fact is — er — ah — well, you see, that is, the skipper never got around to making me a PPC after all. It seems there were a bunch of other officers in the squadron in the same boat with me as concerns total flight time, rank, etc., and he explained to me that he couldn't qualify me without taking in all the others also, and there wasn't time for all that. I didn't push it, as he gave me such a good fitness report — the best in the squadron, because I as Personnel Officer saw the reports on all the officers — that I thought I should be satisfied. After all, the fitness report is what goes to Washington and is the most important thing to me as a naval officer, although the PPC qualification is more important to me as a flier. But I didn't get it yet, so you may consider me as moronic and screwy as before. If you don't mind, darling, I feel better that way. I want to be like you, see. (Wow, wotta shot!)

I will now redeem myself by saying that as a Sweeney, the most important thing to me is you, Beebe.

All my love,
Jack

ESTIMATED DATE OF LEAVING HAWAII	ESTIMATED METHOD OF TRANSPORTATION	ESTIMATED DATE OF ARRIVAL U.S.A.	ESTIMATED PLACE OF ARRIVAL	NO. OF DAYS TILL ESTIMATED B-B DAY
INDEF.	SHIP	INDEF. PLUS 6 DAYS	?	?

My darling,

As you see by the scoreboard at the top of the page (Pat. applied for), things are still sorta hazy. I'm almost sure it won't take them more than another week to get us on some sort of transportation, so the figure in the last box up there, which is the One that matters, shouldn't be more than 15 or 20.

I hope your ardor isn't cooling with all this delay. I don't have any way of knowing because they won't let your letters, of which I'm sure there are many, come through to me except very seldom. The latest one I have is dated June 14 — two weeks ago. Today I got your No. 32, dated June 5 — only took it three weeks.

That was the letter that told me about your friend Peggy being out here. It doesn't look as if I'll have a chance to look her up as you suggested so generously, but really old crumpet I just wouldn't be interested even if your letter had arrived in time. I'll explain this attitude of mine further when I see you. It's not that I have anything against Peggy — although her kiss did seem rather anemic compared to others I got that night from a strange, mysterious, and charming blonde whom I hardly knew at the time but whose destiny, as later events proved, was to be inevitably linked with my own. For the following two days, at least. Don't miss next week's chapter, folks; it's gonna be a <u>lulu!</u>

Yes, I think "Come Rain or Come Shine" is okay, and for the fog you asked about, have no fear, have no worry, tell ya what I'm goner dew. (Pun unintentional, really — I'll bet you mist the point, anyway.) You see, I have discovered a gismo that solves all your problems in a fog. You put it beside you in your car, and even though the fog may be as soup as pea thick, this gismo steers you safely through it to your destination, if any. It's portable, so you can take it out of the car into the house with you, throw it into second gear, and immediately it begins to make a noise like a blonde and whips you up a ham-and-cheese-and-egg-and-bacon-and-lettuce-and-tomato sandwich (on toast) and if you keep it in good condition by lubricating frequently with Old-Fashioneds, it will snuggle up to you on the sofa and take you right out of this world. I call it a Beebe, for no good reason at all, except that maybe it looks like a Beebe, and I wouldn't trade the one I've got for anything else in the world.

Any more questions about fog, or is everything clear now?

Wait till you see my sensational new sport shirt. It was just what my golf game needed — I fired an 86 the first time I put it on.

The weather is perfect here, nearly every day. The days are pretty warm, but I like it that way; and the nights are always clear and cool. By the way — old Saturn may not be with us, as he sets pretty early these days, but Mars is still around and Jupiter is that big bright one right overhead every night about 9. It's the brightest one there is. Just another fact for you to tuck away into that lovely head of yours.

The Palms open-air theatre sounds like the cat's meow to me — I've always liked open-air shows. Is it a Drive-In? If so, we'll have to rent a car and take it in. Wish I hadn't sold the old Blue Blunder Bus now, but how was I to know?

Adios, Marequita Linda. I'll see you in my dreams.

All my love to you,
Jack

ESTIMATED DATE OF LEAVING HAWAII	ESTIMATED METHOD OF TRANSPORTATION	EST. DATE OF ARRIVAL IN U.S.	EST. PLACE OF ARRIVAL	NUMBER OF DAYS TILL B-B ● DAY
INDEF.	SHIP	INDEF. PLUS 6 DAYS	SAN FRANCISCO	12 TO 20

Monday, July 1

Dear Slim,

Are we still paying attention, students? Don't lose interest, because it's always darkest before the dawn. True, time is beginning to drag, every day seems to get longer, but when things are so bad they have to get better and <u>surely</u> they'll get us on a ship soon.

Still no letter from my honya since June 14. It's incredible. Did that snapshot I sent you scare you that badly? Or maybe you're not speaking to me since losing 3 dollars in the Louis-Conn fiasco. (We wuz framed.) But I prefer to think you are still writing merrily away and the mail service has gone ph-ff-f-t again. The days are really long when I don't get that blue letter. I've read your last one — number 32 dated June 5 — over muchas veces and still get a thrill every time I read the part about you not dating anyone recently, because, although I'm not really

152

selfish, I'd hate to think of anyone else having as much fun with you as I did.

As for me, I don't have to tell you how true I've been to you — one reason being that the females have been few and far between ever since I last saw you but the main reason being that I haven't been interested in other fems since I last saw you. Or <u>first</u> saw you, for that matter.

Darling, you've said several times that this was really the first time you've felt that you were in love. That's the most wonderful thing that's ever been told to me, and all I hope is that I'm worthy of it. I wish I could say the same to you — perhaps somebody else in my place would anyway, for fear of losing you, but I always try to put all my cards on the table and it's not in me to lie about something like that. I've been in love twice before, although I'm not sure I ought to count the first time as I was pretty young — 19. Anyway, I <u>thought</u> it was the real thing and I guess that's all that counts. Anyhow, my experience with those two girls, both of whom I regarded as perfect angels (not at the same time, of course), left me with the conviction that no female in this hyar world is to be completely and fully trusted. Present company is, of course, excepted. The third time is supposed to be charming, and it is.

But enuf of my battered and shattered ole heart, I can tell you more better in person, let's get on to less serious things.

Yesterday was a beautiful Sunday (at least the afternoon part was; I wouldn't know about the a.m.) and I spent it the way I like to spend a Sunday afternoon — I watched a baseball game, the first I've seen this year, found a swell little place in Honolulu to eat and had a luscious filet mignon with French fries (no profiterole) and afterwards saw one of the best movies ever made, "Ruggles of Red Gap" with Chas. Laughton; although it <u>was</u> made about ten years ago. I was only 16 then, and plenty cute, kiddo. Come to think of it, you were only 24 then yourself — gee, I'll bet you were beautiful when you were 24.

You probably think you don't like baseball, but

with me there to explain the finer points of the game to you, I'm sure you are going to like it. Especially the hot-dog-and-coke part of it, not to mention the peanuts — all part of the game, dear.

Excuse pliz while I run out to play Ed Mallick a tennis match — he's the second best tennis player here. Will let you know how I come out.

Square shooters always win — namely, me, by a score of 6–4, 6–0.

Feel plenty good now after workout and shower.

My new pay raise goes into effect today, sweetheart — I won't tell you how much it is for fear you will love me only for my money but it's sensational and means I can now afford to buy <u>two</u> sacks of popcorn — one for eating in the lobby and one for the main feature. That isn't inflation — that's improvement in standard of living.

(I could add that the inflation comes in later when you blow up your empty p.c. sack and bust it in your escort's ear — but I won't.) (Unless we're in the balcony.) (And we probably will be.)

Keep thinking of me, sugah. I'll be headin' back to

the bonny bonny banks of Loch Loma one of these days, no foolin'.

All my love.
Jack

P.S. Neither of those two girls was as wonderful as I think you are.

EST. DATE OF LEAVING HAWAII	EST. METHOD OF TRANSPORTATION	EST. DATE ARRIVAL USA	EST. PLACE OF ARRIVAL	EST. NUMBER DAYS TILL B·B·Day
JULY 4	U.S.S. RANDALL (NAVY TRANSPORT SHIP)	JULY 11	SAN FRANCISCO	10

Wednesday, July 3

My darling,

Yippee! Haven't time to write, but have got to do a rapid job of packing so as to get over to Pearl Harbor and get on good ship Randall which leaves 4th of July for San Francisco.

I love youse.

Jack

Will try to call you from S.F.

Mr. and Mrs. Arthur Adelbert Mathewson

announce the marriage of their daughter

Ethel Marie

to

John Milton Sweeney

Lieutenant, United States Navy

on Friday, the twenty sixth of July

nineteen hundred and forty-six

Christ Episcopal Church

Coronado, California

was in love with you. It expla...
f queer things that have been ...
or instance, why I write you ...
letters, why I think about you ...
he day and dream about you ...
he night, ... I'm so eager...
ack to ... your ...
tuition (... ark so ...
rues) you ... it all ...
ugh. And ... great ...
me for y... me any...
which is up to nobody but you...
now I'll never forget anything a...
hose twelve days between ~~Jan~~ Dec. 29...
m. 9 (Check?) Only two months a...
t was that we were in the ...
...l, the Biltmore Bowl, and, a...
ter, the Boysenberry Bowl.

The amazing thing about it ...
...g of coincidences that set up

Part Three

My father met my mother at the tail end of a year and a half spent in navy flight training at the base near Coronado, California, where she lived. The year was 1945. They had known each other for only eleven days when he, then a lieutenant in the United States Navy, left with his flight squadron to report to Hawaii as part of the military's effort to stabilize the Pacific after World War II. Over a period of seven months, he wrote the forty-five letters I found in her drawer.

I loved listening to my mother tell me the story of their courtship. They met on December 29, at a tea party for his navy flight squadron at the Hotel del Coronado, and the next day he called her for their first date. They drove up to Pasadena for the Rose Bowl game and parade. (Jack forgot his map, and

Beebe said she knew the way but didn't.) They spent the next ten days together golfing and playing tennis; in the evenings they went to movies and dancing. The time he had with her before reporting for squadron duty was enough for him to know.

When my father returned to San Diego from the Pacific seven months later, he went directly to my mother's father to ask him for her hand in marriage. My grandfather's response was, "Well, you know Beebe's expensive." My grandmother, hard of hearing, misheard his comment and said, "What? You say Beebe's pregnant?!" My mother always said she "just knew" that Jack was the right one. They were married less than three weeks after he returned in the same small Episcopal church in Coronado where my mother was baptized. They had their reception in the Hotel del Coronado, where they had first met.

How sweet he was to my mother! He fell in love with her, and that was that. I was amazed at how unabashedly romantic he was, and silly, just as I'd seen him in my mind's eye when I was a child. In these letters I discovered a man who was candid, open, sensitive, guileless. My mother must have felt more enchanted with every letter she received. I thought about the kinds of things he might have said to me, his daughter, and the ways in which he would have made me feel unique and loved. I was right to imagine him the way I had. In one of his letters, my father wrote, "You'd know what I meant, but how about the people who'll read this forty years from now in 'Famous Letters of Famous Naval Heroes' compiled by Lt. J. M. Sweeney, USN (Retired)?" I was reading this letter exactly forty years later. It was strange — I suddenly felt his presence acutely. I had had the same feeling the first time I saw his photograph. I could have sworn I saw him grinning.

These letters also introduced me to someone I didn't expect to find: my mother. Bright, energetic, and fun, at twenty-three she was a real beauty. I wish everyone could see their mother at a time in her life when life is still a good proposition, rosy and promising. I wonder if my mother knew how much I would enjoy meeting her in these letters; how happy I would be knowing she was so well loved.

I'm sure my father saved her letters to him, as she did his, and that my mother threw them away when she was packing up the house in Bermuda. How could she have stood at the time to be reminded of her feelings — her hopes and dreams for their future together? It would have been too much.

All kinds of thoughts occurred to me as I read the letters. My father's handwriting was beautiful. So elliptical and soft and gentle. And he seldom doubted himself — few words are crossed out or thoughts reconsidered. It took me a while to figure out why he had supplied my mother with his pronunciation guides, like "Tsingtao Harbor (har-ber)" and "po-kerr." His Texan accent! I don't think my mother had ever left California before she met him, and she may not have ever met a Texan. She probably thought it very funny.

Something else struck me: He kept asking my mother for a photograph, because, he said, "it will serve as an anchor on [his] imagination." I knew exactly what he meant. All my life I'd needed an anchor on my imagination; a full, real picture of my father.

I decided to go to Texas to meet my father's relatives. Mrs. Sweeney, my grandmother, had visited

Coronado several times when I was a child, and I had once met one of my father's brothers, but I didn't know any of his other siblings, and I knew my father had been one of nine children. I wrote to one of his sisters who I knew lived in Breckenridge, Texas, and she wrote back, encouraging me to come to Texas for what she called a "little sentimental journey."

In the spring of 1987 I flew to Dallas and was greeted at the airport by several aunts, who said they recognized me by my resemblance to my father. We drove to Bonham, a small town in east Texas where his family had lived for several generations. I learned he was named John Milton Sweeney not for the English poet, as I had always imagined, but for his grandfather, John Milton Nunn, who had built the first brick house in Bonham in 1871 with handmade bricks imported by oxcart. We drove down to Ladonia, where my father was born. His father, Albert Sweeney, had been president of the bank there until it closed in 1931 following the stock market crash. He refused to declare bankruptcy, and made a settlement with every depositor. I began to get an idea of who the Sweeneys were, their history, and of the events and lessons in my father's childhood that might have informed his life as an adult.

Our trip ended in Breckenridge, a former oil town about one hundred miles west of Fort Worth. During the boom days, oil wells sprouted every few feet in Breckenridge, and its main street was nothing but mud and wooden shacks. By 1931 when the Sweeneys arrived, Breckenridge had become what my grandmother described as "beyond the jumping-off place." Still, she raised her nine children there and grew to love it, living there the rest of her life. When the family first arrived, an eleven-year-old Jack tried to convert the side yard, which was just bare earth and scorched caliche, into a baseball diamond. When he finally had the grass growing, a neighbor commented to my grandmother that her kids were ruining the grass with their baseball games. Mrs. Sweeney pointed out she was raising children, not grass.

In Breckenridge I was given my father's high school yearbooks; he was "Most Popular Boy" in his senior year and "Most Valuable Post-Graduate" the year after high school. I heard over and over again just how much Jack was loved and how his death at such a young age was a great loss to everyone who had known him. I realized, too, that having never met him would always be my loss.

Nothing I heard there made me think he was less than perfect. Still. But a fuller picture began to emerge. Why had he become a navy pilot? Was he anything like the other pilots I had known back in Coronado? One of his sisters told me that his reason for becoming a pilot was very simple. As a turret officer on the USS *Tennessee* during the war, he had left the deck minutes before an explosion onboard killed everyone on deck. This haunted him, and he went to flight school because he did not want to see death at such close hand again. And when the war ended, he said he was happy just to be alive.

After I got back, one of Jack's sisters sent me a letter my mother wrote to Jack's mother after his death.

Coronado, Ca.
Nov. 30th, 1956
Dear Mother,

I tried to call you last nite, just to hear your voice, but had no success in reaching you. Tried til 9:30 your time at Peggy's and then gave up. Anyhoo a letter is better as I have so much to say to you.

As you know, the search was unsuccessful. When you come out here, more on that later, I will show you the many letters the Navy dept. wrote me concerning the flight. Jack just disappeared. Perhaps that was a blessing as he suffered no pain. I just can't put into words how I feel but both you and I have faith in God and perhaps someday I'll understand the "Why."

Mother, Jack fully realized his danger and I firmly believe that the Lord saw to it that he see his loved ones his last few months. He wrote me a letter, which I found in his briefcase, a comforting one in which he said that he has lived a lifetime already. He had done, seen and enjoyed life to the fullest. We had 10½ years together, we loved each other dearly and I have so many happy memories of him.

170

Jack left us well provided for. On the 7th a casualty claim man from the Navy is coming over to handle all the finances from the gov't etc. We have quite a bit of stocks which Jack wants me to convert to long term growth. I and the children have complete free medical care, commissary privileges etc. Also I am entitled to a G.I. loan.

I am looking for a house, a rental one as Jack suggested, but I may have to buy. Nothing is settled, everything takes time. It will take two months for our furniture to arrive so imagine we'll stay with my parents until perhaps the 1st of Feb. I'd like so much to see you but had better wait until I get my finances settled. Perhaps Christmas of 57 we can come or anytime that you'd like us.

In the meantime Jack and I are going to have another baby. Sometime in March I believe. The doctor, whom I saw for the first time Tuesday, the 27th, said I was 5 to 5½ months pregnant. Yes, Jack knew. I am so happy to have one more chance to bear Jack's children. If it's a boy I'm going to call him Joe, Jack always loved that name, but I have no name for a girl — perhaps

171

Mary or Ann. Can you come out here in March or the latter part of February? We'll have our own house by then, I plan to get full time help, but I'd like you with us especially at nights. I would most likely have to go to the hospital at nite, I can go by car and you would be there with the children.

I have John and Bill in school which simplifies my work in the mornings. Billy comes home at noon and John comes home at 3pm. Rudy is wonderful, takes the boys to school in the morning and picks up Billy, takes Al for walks and watches Danny when I have to go out. It won't be hard for you, I'd just like you to be with me during that time. Please come.

Will write you more soon. Danny is awake so had better go.

> All our love always,
> Beebe and the boys

My father had known my mother was pregnant. He had known about me. This was all I needed to know.

. . .

My mother could always make me laugh. Once I'd spent too much time at the beach and was suffering from massive sunburn. My ankles were swollen, and I could only walk hunched over and with great effort. Every time she looked at me she burst into laughter. She called me Quasimodo. She had names for everyone. She nicknamed my ever-faithful and gallant college boyfriend Lochinvar, when it became clear he loved to help out, always grabbing a paintbrush before anyone else. Whenever she'd find me comfortably sprawled out on the couch with a book, she'd say, "Well, position isn't everything in life."

In the course of a few years, I watched as my mother grew weaker and weaker from heart disease. She tried hard to get used to the oxygen tubes she was hooked up to. I remember once holding her by the arm, trying to help her settle into a chair. She said, a bit impatiently, "Let go of me, I'm fine." I let go and she collapsed backward into the chair, startling both of us. She looked up at me, smiled, and said, "I didn't want it to be this way. I wanted to go out swinging." I can't help remembering her this way — stoic, feisty, even funny.

After my mother's death, I hired a boat in Mission Bay to take her ashes out to the Pacific Ocean. I told the captain of the boat I wanted to go around Point Loma so I could scatter her ashes in the waters off Coronado. He said he never went that far out to sea, and besides, he was sure he didn't have enough fuel. I think I begged him and agreed to pay him extra. I wouldn't scatter my mother's ashes anywhere else.

As the boat cut through the water, the fog that had been so heavy earlier in the morning began to dissipate. I thought of my mother describing that fog as "June gloom." You can count on the fog rolling out to sea by noon and the sun shining through. That's what it was like that day. As we rounded Point Loma, the sun became bright overhead and I could see Coronado Beach across the ocean, where I'd spent time as a young child with my mother. I loved standing in front of her, waiting excitedly for each new wave to roll in. Just as each wave reached the shore, she would grab me and lift me above it. I leaned over the side of the boat and threw the ashes overboard. I thought back to the day I sat on the beach with my friend, wondering where my father was. The oceans connect, somehow. He is out there. Still.

My father's last letter to my mother was written shortly before he died. I have since learned more about that night. His plane went down about four hundred miles north of Bermuda. Pilots in his squadron remember the long flying hours in November of 1956; they were on war-alert status because of the Suez Canal crisis. My father's plane, a Martin Marlin P5M, was loaded with explosives and on a mission to search for Russian submarines in the Atlantic.

On the evening of November 9, a freighter radioed a report of having seen a plane crash into the sea about four miles away and explode. It also reported the brief appearance of a light on a life raft before it lost sight of it in heavy squalls and darkness. After about twenty-five minutes a second explosion was heard, as the depth charges the plane was carrying went off. The navy and coast guard searched for several days, but nothing of the plane or the crew was ever found.

My father's plane did not disappear in the

Bermuda Triangle while he was on a simple milk run to Pensacola. It would, of course, have been much easier to believe that he had quietly slipped down to the bottom of the ocean rather than die in a fiery crash. As it turns out, my father did die in a war — the Cold War — although it was a war none of us even knew we were fighting. What we were told at the time was typical of the kind of vague and shadowy story the navy passed down to families left behind. I know that it is only through my own relentless search for my father that I finally learned the truth of what happened to him on November 9, 1956.

I still wonder what it was that prompted my father to write that one last letter to my mother. Perhaps in the war-alert atmosphere, the thought of dying was unavoidable. It is a question I will never have an answer to. But it's a letter I'm very lucky to have.

He writes, "As long as I'm remembered, I'm not really dead." Through his courtship letters my father is remembered, and probably just as he should be. He is remembered as a young naval officer crazy in love. He's twenty-six years old and he's going to marry a beautiful California blonde he's known less than six months. They'll have five children, though he won't live to see them grow up. He'll die serving his country. But he will be remembered because he's not really dead. Not to me, anyway. He never was.

Bermuda

November 1956

To the best wife a man ever had:

Honey, I am writing this letter to you to say a few things that I might leave unsaid if I should depart this world unexpected-like. In this flying business you never can tell when you might all of a sudden get mighty unlucky and wake up dead some morning.

I suppose this shows me up for the old sentimental fool I have always been, but I thought if I could make sure you know how I feel about such things it might be a little comfort to you.

First of all, let's face one fact — everybody ends up dead. Think of all the infants and children and people who had the misfortune to die before they got very much of anything out of life, and then think of all I got out of it.

Even if I should die the day after writing this, I still claim I am one of the luckiest people who ever lived, and you know it. I've got a lot to live for, as I write this, but when I count up all the blessings I've had, I can see that I have already lived a lot. When you come right down to it, I've done just about everything I've wanted

178

to do and seen about everything I've wanted to see. Sure, I'd like to stick around while the boys are growing up. But you and I agree so closely on how to raise a family, the boys are going to be all right; I'm sure of that. And I've had enough fun with you to last anybody a lifetime.

Don't let the memories of me keep you from marrying again, if you run across somebody fit to be your husband, which would be hard to find, I know. But you're much too wonderful a wife and mother to waste yourself as a widow. Life is for the living. (That's not original, I'm sure.)

So get that smile back on your face, put on some lipstick and a new dress, and show me what you can do toward building a new life. Just remember me once in a while — not too often, or it'll cramp your style, you know — and as long as I'm remembered, I'm not really dead. I'll still be living in John, and Bill, and Al, and Dan, bless their hearts. That's what they mean by eternity, I think.

My love as always,
Jack

ACKNOWLEDGMENTS

There are several people I wish to thank, beginning with Julia, Peggy, Jim, Ede Pi, and Anita Sweeney. My thanks also to Andrew Carroll, and Miriam Altshuler; my father's Annapolis classmate Al Rasmussen; and Mac McDermott, Roger Straus III, and Emily Lewis. I'm grateful to Bob Griffin and Lou Marrero of VPNavy-49 and to Colin Pomeroy, author of *The Flying Boats of Bermuda,* who provided me with information regarding my father's plane crash. My thanks to my editor, Deborah Baker, and to Michael Pietsch and Pamela Marshall, and, in fact, everyone at Little, Brown; they have shown the kind of enthusiasm for this book that an author dreams of. Finally, my love and gratitude to Wendy Weil, Ann Torrago, and Emily Forland at the Wendy Weil Agency.